Paestum

NEW ASPECTS OF ANTIQUITY

General Editor: COLIN RENFREW

Consulting Editor for the Americas: JEREMY A. SABLOFF

JOHN GRIFFITHS PEDLEY

Paestum

Greeks and Romans in Southern Italy

with 136 illustrations, 11 in color

THAMES AND HUDSON

For George and Annie
and for Mary

Frontispiece: A pair of maidens from a surviving metope of the Temple in the sanctuary at Foce del Sele.

First published in the USA in 1990 by
Thames and Hudson Inc.,
500 Fifth Avenue, New York, New York 10110

Library of Congress Catalog Card Number 89-51868

Printed in Singapore

CONTENTS

GENERAL EDITOR'S FOREWORD

It is one of the paradoxes of classical antiquity that some of the finest of the Greek temples are to be found outside Greece. Sicily boasts a remarkable series, some of them still standing: at Agrigento, on the south, with its splendid 'Temple of Concord' along with the remains of several others; at Selinunte, further west, where there is another group; a splendid, unfinished building at Segesta; and in some ways the most memorable, at Syracuse, the Temple of Athena, a large part of which is incorporated into the medieval cathedral. But Magna Graecia, 'Great Greece', included also much of peninsular Italy, south of Rome. And it is at Paestum, some 50 miles (80 km) down the coast from Naples, that there stands what many have considered the finest complex of temples to survive from the ancient world.

As Professor Pedley makes clear, in his lucid account, they were slow to attract the fame that is now rightly theirs. Perhaps their unhealthy malaria-infested environs deterred the traveller in the eighteenth and nineteenth centuries (they are now happily free of this hazard), although they were studied and drawn by that great arbiter of classical taste Piranesi.

Yet the city of Paestum has much more to offer than these three astonishingly well-preserved monuments. Already established by colonists from Sybaris towards the end of the seventh century BC, the city took some of its present form in the sixth century. The Roman colony was founded in 273 BC, and on top of the Greek remains is the well-laid-out Roman city with some 3 miles (4.8 km) of town walls, armed with towers. Aerial photography has established that the whole city is there, awaiting investigation, although excavations have so far covered only a limited area.

In his account, John Pedley reviews not only the Italian work in the city, and the work of the German Archeological Institute on the study and conservation of the temples, but his own work (along with American and Italian colleagues) at the *località* Santa Venera, in a sanctuary close to the south wall of the city. His account gives a clear picture of the early Greek city, of its later years, of the heyday of the Roman colony which succeeded it, and of the early medieval period and its aftermath.

The cemeteries are among the important finds at the site, including painted tombs which bear comparison with their more famous counterparts at Tarquinia, in Etruria, to the north of Rome. Those of Paestum, however, while they may show some Etruscan influence, belong within the Greek world ('Magna Graecia' is no misnomer), and they contain some of the finest paintings to survive from it.

Yet when all is said and done, the great joys of the site are those three splendid temples, built following the Doric order. The so-called 'Basilica' dates from the middle of the sixth century, and nearby is the excellently preserved 'Temple of Poseidon' dating from *c.* 450 BC, and probably dedicated to Hera. To the north lies the smaller 'Temple of Ceres' (in reality probably dedicated to Athena). Together they form a wonderfully impressive group, and Professor Pedley's authoritative account of them brings out well both their originality and their place firmly within the mainstream of the Greek architectural tradition. It offers, at the same time, a valuable insight into the work of modern classical archaeology.

Colin Renfrew

PREFACE

Interest in Paestum has gathered pace over the last twenty or so years, stimulated partly by challenging new archaeological finds, of which the painted Tomb of the Diver may have been the most eye-catching, and by the growth of tourism generally. More and more people visit the city every year; and if their interest is directed first and foremost to the surprisingly well-preserved Greek temples, it rapidly encompasses also the surviving remains of the Roman town: forum, houses, baths and streets. The museum at the site was built originally to house the sculpted stone blocks (metopes, to give them their technical name) from the sixth century BC buildings in the sanctuary of Hera at the mouth of the river Sele just north of Paestum proper; it still amazes for the richness of its holdings both of relief sculpture and of wall-painting of Greek and Lucanian times. Here too interest has been easily engaged and is growing all the time.

This new and energetic interest in the ancient city has led to this book. My first thanks go then to those who made this interest possible: to Pellegrino Sestieri, Mario Napoli and Friedrich Krauss who first gave serious and prolonged thought to the city and its significance, and to Paola Zancani-Montuoro and Umberto Zanotti-Bianco whose discovery and publication of the Heraion at Foce del Sele opened new avenues of research. All recent archaeological work builds on the framework erected by these scholars, and all recent interest, scholarly and otherwise, stems from their work. My second thanks go to those who exemplify the current enthusiasm for the city and its environs: to Werner Johannowsky and Giuliana Tocco Sciarelli, past and present Superintendents of Antiquities within whose province Paestum stands; to Angelo Ardovino, Laura Rota and Marina Cipriani, past and present Directors of the Archaeological Museum of Paestum; to Antonella Fiammenghi and Giovanni Avagliano, officers of the Superintendency working constantly in and around the site; and to Emmanuele Greco and Dinu Theodorescu whose enterprising and skilful work within the city walls is radically altering our understanding of the topography of the city and refining earlier chronologies. I am particularly grateful to colleagues from the University of Perugia through whose agency and ingenuity my own interest in Paestum was fostered: to Mario Torelli, Gianpiero Pianu and Concetta Masseria whose keenness for Paestum is matched only by their knowledge. The extent of the contributions of all these scholars is only partially reflected in the bibliography at the end of this book.

Participants in the Michigan-Perugia excavations in the extramural sanctuary in the *località* Santa Venera made possible the contents of Chapter Eight: Jim Higginbotham, Gail Hoffman, Meg Morden, Theresa Menard, Rebecca Miller (Ammerman), Ann van Rosevelt, Gianpiero Pianu, Concetta Masseria, Marina Pinna, Rachel Vargas, Monica Barran, Andrea Berlin, Carol Stein, and Mary-Ann Eaverly all laboured long hours in various capacities. Antonio Taddeo, Vincenzo DiBartolomeo, Antonio Ciervo, Giuseppe DeFiore, Carmine Federico, Cosimo Federico, another Cosimo Federico, Arturo LaCorte, Luigi Pinto, Ferdinando Marino and Carmine Di Biasi contributed with equal vigour and success. Ezio Mitchell, David Myers and Jackie Royer drew the plans, elevations, and sections; Aaron Levin, Betty Naggar and Sue Webb took the photographs; Al Ammerman and Jan Sevink interpreted the geology, Sharon Herbert the pottery, Ted Buttrey the coins, David Reese the bones, and Jane Waldbaum the metal objects. I am grateful to them all.

In Ann Arbor, maps and plans were drawn by David Bosse and Mary Pedley; Marj Ramsbotham and Lisa Hansen struggled to produce a legible manuscript from my errorprone pages. In London, Thames and Hudson's anonymous reader made many helpful suggestions as did their editorial staff. I thank them all.

I hope the book presents an accurate picture of the growth and development of a Greek city in South Italy. I hope too that I have done justice to Paestum's archaeological riches, and to those scholars, students, enthusiasts and local people whose lives have been enriched, as mine has, by thinking about a community which flourished so many centuries ago.

INTRODUCTION

They stand between the mountains and the sea:
Awful memorials, but of whom we know not!
Italy, A Poem
Samuel Rogers (1830)

Early History

The ancient Greek city of Poseidonia, better known perhaps by its Roman
name of Paestum, is located towards the southern end of the Bay of Salerno,
some 20 miles (32 km) south of the Amalfi coast and 50 miles (80 km) south
of Naples. It lies approximately 640 m from the present-day coastline on a
low limestone ridge which dictated the polygonal line of the city's fortification
wall. This defensive system, consisting of walls, towers and gates, and
running about 3 miles (4.8 km) in length, is remarkably preserved – though
with some modifications in antiquity and some restoration more recently –
and is an imposing sight. Yet it is hardly as impressive as the three
Greek temples, upstanding emblems, remarkably preserved, of architectural
creativity and religious fervour. About the life of the Greek city, which was
founded about 600 BC and flourished for two hundred years, the literary
sources are mute. The archaeology is all important.

About 400 BC Poseidonia fell victim to the Italic peoples of the interior,
who in the fifth century began a series of campaigns against the Greek cities;
in Poseidonia the new masters were called Lucanians. They lasted, on and
off, for the best part of a century and a half until, in the great expansion of
imperializing Rome, a Latin colony was planted here in 273 BC and the city's
name was changed to Paestum. The city then embarked upon an architectural
elaboration which yielded all the forms of a typical Roman town – *cardo*
and *decumanus* (the major roads), Forum, temple, *comitium* (meeting
place for political debate), amphitheatre, domestic housing. Yet the Greek
sanctuaries continued, and the city is, in short, an astonishing capsule of
classical antiquity with Greek and Roman buildings side by side.

The Monuments

Visible today are not only the fortification walls, begun in the Greek period
and completed by the Romans, and the Greek temples, two of the sixth and
one of the fifth century BC, but also several Greek monumental altars, a
votive column of Greek date, and the Greek *bouleuterion* or *ekklesiasterion*,

1 Map of South Italy and Sicily. In the Greek period, Paestum was called Poseidonia.

2 Aerial view of the central zone of the city, seen from the north. The sanctuary and temple of Athena appear in the foreground with the Forum and temples of Hera beyond. The sanctuary in the località *Santa Venera and the Cirio factory, are visible to the upper left.*

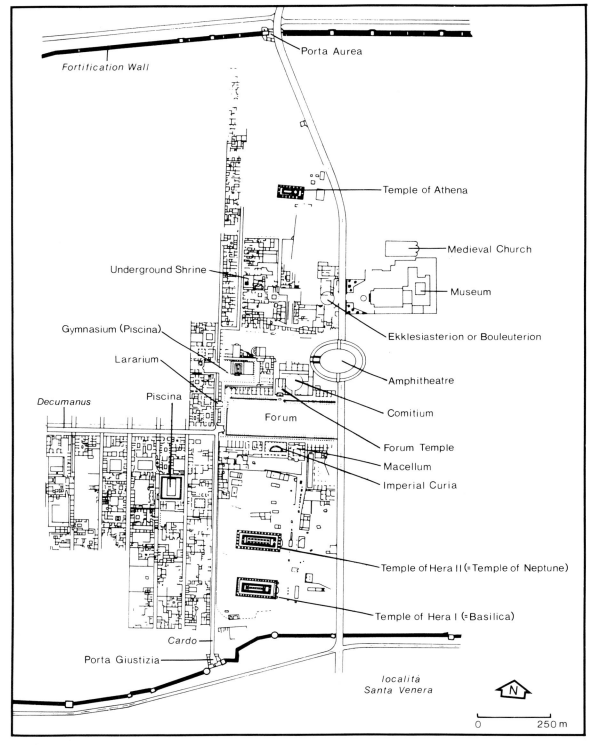

Porta Aurea

Fortification Wall

Temple of Athena

Medieval Church

Underground Shrine

Museum

Ekklesiasterion or Bouleuterion

Gymnasium (Piscina)

Lararium

Amphitheatre

Piscina

Comitium

Decumanus

Forum

Forum Temple

Macellum

Imperial Curia

Temple of Hera II (= Temple of Neptune)

Temple of Hera I (= Basilica)

Cardo

Porta Giustizia

*località
Santa Venera*

N

0   250 m

3 *Plan of the excavated area within the city walls, showing roads, sections of the city walls, and ancient and
modern buildings.*

a structure in which democratic political debate took place. There is also a mysterious semi-underground Greek cultic building in which were found 8 bronze vessels containing honey, and, among other materials, an Athenian vase of the late sixth century BC, all now in the Museum.

Most of what the visitor sees, however, though less striking than the temples, is of Roman date. The Forum, a rectangular space measuring *c.* 57 × 150 m, with the eastern end disappearing beneath the modern road, is bounded by porticoes, shops and by important public buildings: a major civic temple improbably identified by scholars as the *capitolium* (and if so dedicated to Jupiter, Juno and Minerva) faces from the north; the *comitium*, the place of assembly for the election of magistrates, is directly adjacent to the temple; more public buildings flank the south side. The western part of the amphitheatre – the eastern again is buried beneath the modern road – is visible nearby to the north; as is a huge *gymnasium/piscina* (swimming pool) now thought perhaps to be of cultic significance. The *cardo maximus*, the main north-south highway of the Roman city, is in plain view, a cobbled artery deeply rutted by cart and chariot wheels, one may suppose, all the way from the southern gate of the city to the *compitum*, the central crossroads; there, directly to the west of the Forum, it meets the *decumanus*, the main east-west route across the city. The *cardo* may be traversed in long stretches to the north, the *decumanus* to the west, and it is easy to see here the dogmatic rectilinearity of ancient town planning and the city blocks and housing which are its component parts.

The Museum houses the objects retrieved in the excavations: votive terracotta figures, ivory statuettes and plaques, gold and silver jewellery and disks, a vast range of plain and decorated pottery. Dazzling are the wall paintings of Greek and Lucanian date which decorated the interior of tombs and allow a glimpse of what domestic interiors may have looked like. Most spectacular is the facsimile of the Treasury from the sanctuary of Hera at Foce del Sele, some 5.5 miles (8.5 km) to the north of the city proper; justly famous for its sculpted stone metopes – rectangular blocks decorating the superstructure – this gallery of relief figures depicting the exploits of legendary Greek heroes is alone worth the journey to Paestum.

Later History

Aerial photographs of the city taken prior to the landings of American troops in 1943 show the street plan of the Roman town beneath the earth, the Greek temples, and the city wall with great clarity; they also show how relatively little archaeological work had been done. In fact, the site has been amazingly isolated since antiquity. Following the contraction of the population from the first century AD onwards, the Greek temple of Athena was later converted to a Christian basilica, and a medieval village grew up around it. Another basilica too was built, the church of Santa Maria

4 *Aerial view of the city showing the polygonal line of the fortification walls, the modern highway bisecting the city north-south, the gridlike street plan visible beneath the soil, the Salso (Capodifiume) stream skirting the south wall, and the Cirio factory within the* località *Santa Venera by the side of the modern road outside the city to the south.*

dell'Annunziata close by the site of the modern Archaeological Museum, while much of the population moved to the hills and settled Capaccio Vecchio, whence it was – and is – still possible to see the ancient city.

Close by Capaccio Vecchio, another church was dedicated during the eighth century to the Madonna of the Pomegranate. This madonna, with pomegranate in hand, preserves the iconography of the Greek goddess Hera, to whom two of the three Greek temples are dedicated. Moreover, just as processions honouring the Madonna of the Pomegranate carry models of boats today, so archaic terracotta figurines of the Hera of Argos hold model boats full of flowers. Thus do the Greek religious motifs continue, underscoring the imposition of Christianity on ancient cult.

5 View of the city from the north gate, according to Thomas Major (engraving of 1768). In fact the view is from the east gate, showing the two temples of Hera, and the temple of Athena, coyly displayed through a convenient opening in the wall of the gate. Major's engravings drew on many sources and juxtaposed romantic and scientific elements.

Though there was some quarrying, also in the Middle Ages, of the ancient site for buildings at Amalfi and Salerno, thereafter the city was lost in obscurity even during the Renaissance. Although it appears on sea charts of the eighteenth century and therefore functioned as a landmark for navigators, it was not until about the middle of the century that a dignitary of the Neoplitan court, a Count Gazzola, announced the 'discovery' of the temples. A number of scholars and travellers visited at about the same time, among them Thomas Major whose *The Ruins of Paestum otherwise Poseidonia in Magna Graecia* published in London, appeared in 1768. Two kings, of England and Poland, and a brace of dukes were among those who subscribed to Major's volume; in his opening remarks he expressed the hope 'that the present work will fully shew the state of Grecian Architecture in its Infancy, and from thence we may trace the Steps of its progressive Improvements to that Elegance, Grandeur and Magnificence which has been the Admiration of the succeeding Ages.' The renaissance of Doric Architecture in Italy was under way. At the very beginning of his book, he acknowledges his debt to the work of Jacques-Germain Soufflot, the influential French architect. In the following year, 1769, Gabriel Dumont published a similar volume to Major's in Paris in which he claimed obscurely that 'M. Thomas Major a negligé d'indiquer cette source' and implied that the earliest drawings of the temples had been made by Soufflot as early as 1750. In fact there had been earlier visitors than Soufflot and Gazzola: G. Gatta published a somewhat fantastic plan of the city in 1735, and after the opening of the excavations at Herculaneum in 1738 and at Pompeii in 1748, it was inevitable that Paestum should soon catch the eye. Yet, when François Lenormant, the noted French archaeologist, visited the city in the 1880s, almost 40 percent of the coastal plain was covered in huge oak forests, infested by bandits, and it was still a tough ride from Salerno to Paestum. Swamps also discouraged travellers, and Lenormant found that even in September Paestum was deserted for fear of malaria.

Excavations

Land drainage and cultivation schemes only began to take effect at the beginning of this century and little archaeological work was done prior to the pioneering efforts of Vittorio Spinazzola in the early decades of this century. Spinazzola exposed a length of the *cardo maximus* near the South Gate, trenched close to the basilica (= first temple of Hera, or of Hera and Zeus), found prehistoric materials near the Great Altar of the temple, and began the exploration of the south side of the Forum. His work was followed in the 1930s by that of Antonio Marzullo and Amedeo Maiuri, and that of Friedrich Krauss. Marzullo and Maiuri paid particular attention to the city walls, the gates and the main thoroughfares, to the zone around the Temple of Athena, and to the north side of the Forum, while Krauss tackled the

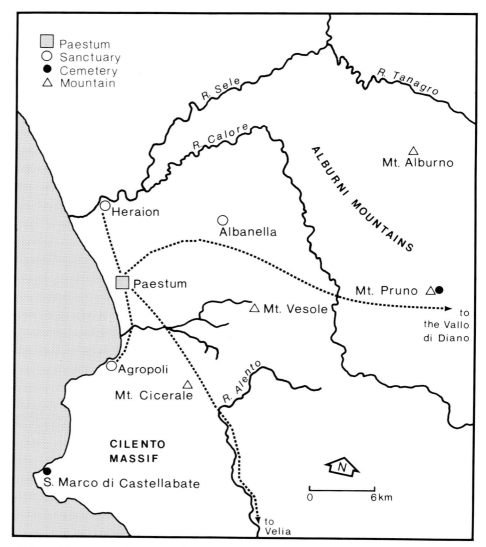

6 Map of Paestum and territory showing rivers, mountains and principal routes. The sanctuaries at the mouth of the river Sele (Heraion) and at Agropoli, which marked the northern and southern boundaries of the chora (the plain), are shown, as is the more recently discovered rural sanctuary at Albanella.

other temples. In the same decade Paola Zancani-Montuoro and Umberto Zanotti-Bianco discovered the sanctuary of Hera at Foce del Sele. Yet the detailed revelation of the whole of the interior of the city, as it is seen today, was the work in the 1950s of Pellegrino Sestieri whose energy and enthusiasm were also responsible for the excavation of necropoleis and other archaeological sites beyond the city's walls. In the 1960s Mario Napoli paid special attention to the cemeteries and was responsible for the sensational discovery of the Greek painted tomb known as the *Tomba del Tuffatore* (Tomb of the Diver); he also masterminded the great project of work now going forward under the leadership of Emanuele Greco and Dinu Theodorescu.

In spite of much removal of earth and a number of erudite interpretations, this city – sequentially Greek, Lucanian and Roman – has remained until recently largely understudied and undervalued. Yet the archaeological record now suggests that this was one of the more important colonies in Magna Graecia, and that it enjoyed its greatest prosperity in the period of the Greek occupation. At the northern edge of Greek colonization in Italy, it stood in close contact with the native populations of the interior and with the Etruscans, a few kilometres to the north, beyond the river Sele; it also stood at the end of an overland route, allowing Greek goods coming from the South to avoid the long sea haul around the toe of Italy and through the straits of Messina. Ample evidence of this trade route may be found at sites like Sala Consilina in the Vallo di Diano, traversed by the river Tanagro, where many Greek objects of the sixth century BC have come to light. The more direct route from Poseidonia to the Vallo di Diano led across the river Calore and close by the site at Monte Pruno (Roscigno) where a rich burial found in 1938 yielded many Greek goods. Pivotal for trade and communications, it is hardly surprising that the city should have achieved eminence.

Poseidonia was well known in antiquity to the denizens of South Italy from the time of the earliest Greek settlement to the end of the Roman era. For most people today however Greece means Athens, Sparta, Delphi, Olympia, Crete, Rhodes. The westward expansion of Greeks to the colonies in Sicily and South Italy, the military, economic and intellectual excitement that went with those daring voyages, and the translation of that boldness into cultural endeavours is sometimes overlooked. The Greeks in the West neither wished to be separated from, nor to be dependent on, their homelands; they drew on information and ideas learnt in Greece itself, but, as Greeks did everywhere, they transformed what they had learned. In the West, experimentation and novelty were the rule; there is great bravado and energy about building programs, about sculptural innovations and developments, and about commercial exchange. Above all, there is a sense of speed, space, and confidence, and it is cities like Poseidonia which exemplified these trends.

Recent Archaeological Work

Recent work inside the city has focused on stratigraphic and topographical studies which have aimed at refining and reinterpreting the results of earlier work. E. Greco and D. Theodorescu have already published three volumes of their important research: *Poseidonia-Paestum* I (Rome 1980) on the zone including the south side of the Forum, *Poseidonia-Paestum* II (Rome 1983) on the area south of the Temple of Athena, the *agora*, and *Poseidonia-Paestum* III (Rome 1986) on the area including the north and west sides of the Forum. Their work continues. Dieter Mertens of the German Archaeological Institute has been engaged in a project of restoration and conservation of the temples, and he and colleagues from the Institute have now undertaken a new study of the walls, towers and gates of the city; their work is currently in progress.

Outside the city, a thoroughgoing investigation of the sanctuary close to the south wall in the *località* Santa Venera was carried out between 1981 and 1985 by the Universities of Michigan and Perugia, and by the Soprintendenza. The resumption of work begun by Sestieri was prompted by a number of reasons: 1) the size and setting of the sanctuary suggested the presence of a major state cult; 2) the retrieval of votive terracottas in the earlier excavations suggested continuity of use of the sanctuary from Greek into Roman times; and 3) the highly unusual architectural forms revealed by Sestieri argued that unusual ritual activity was afoot. Preliminary reports of the work have appeared in the *American Journal of Archaeology* for 1983, 1984 and 1985, and the first volume of the final publication is in press. Greek *necropoleis* to the north and northwest of the city (Arcioni, Ponte di Ferro) were excavated in 1976–78 and in 1983–84 under the auspices of the Soprintendenza, and systematic enquiry has been pushed forward in the large cemetery to the south of the city in the *località* Santa Venera since 1982.

Further afield, but within the territory of the city, and again under the auspices of the Soprintendenza, important work, begun in 1979 and recently completed (1985) at Albanella, some 10 miles (16 km) northeast of the city has revealed a rural sanctuary dedicated to Demeter and Kore. In 1983 excavation on the acropolis at Agropoli, in cramped circumstances, revealed materials (which included architectural terracottas similar to those of the basilica at Poseidonia) going back to the sixth century and beyond; while in the same year Roman tombs of the imperial period were the object of intense scrutiny by the Soprintendenza at S. Marco di Castellabate.

Work of retrieval, analysis, distillation and synthesis goes forward and was crowned by the 1987 international Convegno degli Studi sulla Magna Grecia at Taranto, which took Paestum as the focus of its deliberations.

CHAPTER ONE

THE GREEK WESTWARD EXPANSION

Precursors

Homer's depiction of the adventures of Odysseus represents on one level, commentators say, psychological journeys pertinent to Everyman: the encounter with the Lotus-Eaters mirrors the battle with inertia and indolence, that with Circe the struggle with the dread power of sex. On another level, the dangers of Odysseus' wanderings suggest episodes of heroic life in Greece during the Dark Ages. Certainly, the story of long voyages in desperate conditions would have evoked trenchant memories in the minds of itinerant Greeks of the eighth and seventh centuries BC.

The forebears of the Greeks who left their homelands to found colonies in the late eighth and seventh centuries were the Late Bronze Age Mycenaeans. Travelling eastward and southward, these ironless adventurers made their presence felt in Crete, Egypt, the Levant and Asia Minor. Mycenaean goods are found in burials in Egypt, Egyptian goods in graves in Greece; Mycenaean pottery made its way to Ugarit in the Levant and inland in Asia Minor to Sardis and Stratonikeia. Bronze Age Greek navigators also came to the West; to the Lipari Islands, and especially to Tarentum, inside the heel of Italy, where large concentrations of Mycenaean pottery have been found. Further north, sherds of Mycenaean wares at Poseidonia hardly bespeak the presence of late Bronze Age Greeks; but they do prove contacts between early denizens of Poseidonia and the Mycenaean world.

At the end of the Bronze Age civilization collapsed. Death, destruction and abandonment visited the Mycenaean citadels in Greece; the surviving population scattered to the coasts and hills; some even fled abroad to found new settlements in Asia Minor at places like Smyrna and Colophon. In the silence which followed, residents in Greece began new burial customs, made new pottery shapes decorated in new spare styles; iron appeared. The recovery was slow, and took a century or two to manifest itself; but the population began to expand rapidly by *c.* 800 BC, and Greeks were soon taking to the seas again.

Revival in the East

The Greek renaissance was afoot; and commercial and intellectual curiosity were sparked above all by contact with Egypt and the East. It was not long before Greeks established themselves at Al Mina in Syria, finding in oriental goods great reservoirs of capital gain, imagistic power, and cerebral ferment. It was Euboeans who first started the great adventure (at Al Mina), but they were soon joined by Greeks from Asia Minor, the Cyclades and the Mainland traversing the Mediterranean in search of profit, land, and new ideas. In the course of the seventh and sixth centuries, oriental and Egyptian ideas flowed rapidly into the Greek world: writing reappeared in chaotic local scripts; Greek prose and poetry came to life; new techniques of working raw materials resulted in a new architecture, new metallurgy, and a new sculpture; the mythological past and oriental decorative motifs appeared on the surfaces of pots, bronzes, ivories, and terracotta plaques. Commercial life was fostered by the introduction of coinage.

Nowhere was the renaissance more keenly felt than in the Greek communities of Asia Minor. Here were the experiments which led to the formulation of the Ionic order of architecture with its distinctive details of base, column, capital and superstructure (Samos, Ephesus) and of its Aeolic counterpart (Larisa, Neandria, Smyrna, Mytilene); here were the first philosophical schools (Miletus, Teos); here the beginnings of personal poetry (Lesbos, Colophon), here experiments in music (Sardis), here coinage made its appearance perhaps under the aegis of the Lydian kings (Sardis), and here workshops of potpainters (Rhodes) who if less imaginative than their Mainland counterparts, played an important role in passing oriental ideas to Greece proper. And here too, on Samos, flourished marble sculptors who made the representation of the female type, the *kore*, their particular forte.

But it had not all been easy. Greeks had been moved to go abroad not only by trade and curiosity; overpopulation combined with drought, famine and oligarchical systems of land tenure had too been powerful motivators. Herodotos tells us not only of the eager Kolaios setting off for the far West in search of minerals, but also of the wretched Battus and his colleagues, chosen by lot, driven from Thera by starvation and their fellow citizens. The first contacts outside Greece had been with the Orient; but other points of the compass beckoned. Delphi told the stammering Battus to go south to Libya, which he reluctantly did. The Milesians explored the Black Sea to the north. It was again the energetic Euboeans who first moved west; they established themselves at Naxos on the east coast of Sicily, and at Zancle and Rhegium astride the straits of Messina protecting their northward route to another settlement at Pithekoussai in contact with the Etruscans, rich in metals.

The Westward Movement

News of the Eldorado in the west travelled fast, and the Euboeans were soon joined in Sicily and Italy by other groups of Greeks. The route was unexceptional, following the western coast of Greece northward beyond

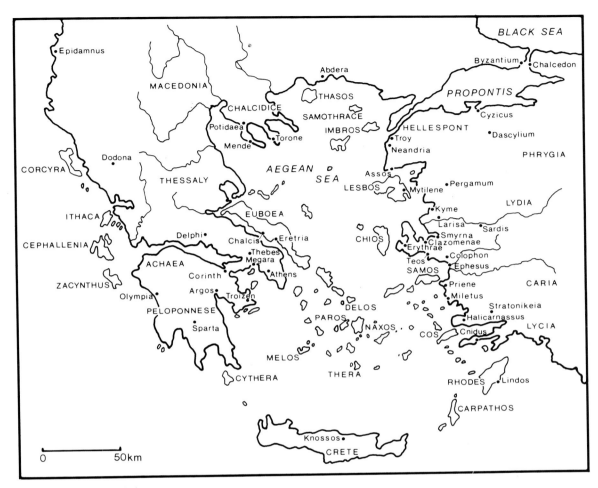

7 Map of Greece and the Aegean coasts.

Corcyra and Epidamnus to a point in modern-day Albania from where the crossing of the Adriatic to the Italian shore was shortest – a route followed even today by Albanian fishermen peddling their catch in Italian markets.

Hugging the coastline first southward and then westward, emigrés from Corinth crossed from Italy to Sicily and settled themselves in the east of the island at Syracuse, soon to become the richest of the western communities. Others came from as far afield as the island of Rhodes, and linked up with other emigrants from Crete to found Gela on the south coast of the island. In Italy too, the pattern of joint ventures was pursued; Achaeans from the northern Peloponnese joined with Troizenians from the Argolid to found Sybaris. Here too there is the only colonial enterprise mounted from Laconia. Spartiates returning home from the protracted first Messenian War, fought and won before the end of the eighth century, discovered – so the story by Antiochos of Syracuse and by Ephoros of Kyme goes – a new generation of children borne from irregular unions in their absence. The Spartan women had let it be known that with all the men away the future of Sparta herself was at stake; accordingly, the youngest warriors had been sent back home. Infants subsequently appeared. These offspring, blessed with the ironic sobriquet of *partheniai* (= the sons of the virgins), were not accorded full civic rights; indignantly they hatched a plot against the state. Betrayed, they were, on the oracular advice of Delphi, banished to Italy where they established themselves at Satyrion and Tarentum.

The northernmost outpost was at Cumae, a mainland site close to Pithekoussai. Here again, some evidence suggests a collaborative foundation. On the one hand, the pottery attests a thoroughgoing Euboean presence among the first settlers; given the proximity to Pithekoussai it would be surprising if this were not the case. On the other hand Pseudo-Skymnos (Skymnos of Chios) reports a tradition suggesting the foundation of Cumae from Kyme in Asia Minor. So, Cumae also may have been founded jointly by Euboeans and other refugees from Kyme in Asia Minor.

The date of the foundation of the settlements depends in the first place on the evidence of Thucydides, and, in the second, on sherds of pottery of Corinthian manufacture found from lowest levels at excavated sites. Pleasingly enough, though there are minor discrepancies and not all scholars agree, the pottery evidence chimes neatly for the most part, with Thucydides. It seems that Cumae was one of the first foundations on the Italian mainland *c.* 740 BC, and Naxos the earliest in Sicily *c.* 735 BC closely followed by Syracuse in *c.* 733 BC; the earliest of all was on the island of Ischia at Pithekoussai, perhaps as early as *c.* 770 BC. Zancle and Rhegium were first settled *c.* 720 BC, Sybaris also *c.* 720 BC, while Tarentum greeted the exiles from Sparta sometime in the last decade of the eighth century. Greeks arrived at Gela in *c.* 688 BC.

The settlers were adept at choosing their new homesteads, and the criteria they used are easy to recognize whether a settlement was in Asia Minor, North Africa or the West. At the first, water, an anchorage, and agricultural land were paramount requirements, while the proclivities of the settlers decided priorities. At Cumae, a trading post, land was not so important; at Gela, an anchorage was of little account, and land was the thing. Islands and peninsulas offering shelter from storms from varying directions were of obvious interest (Pithekoussai).

Syracuse is a conspicuous example. According to Thucydides, Corinthians arrived here in *c.* 733 BC; and the chronology provided by pottery from the lowest excavated levels is consistent with this date. They would not have believed their eyes: an island, a large anchorage, a smaller anchorage and abundant water. They settled on the island (Ortygia); the great harbour to the west was almost circular in shape, 5 miles (8 km) in circumference and almost totally enclosed, while the smaller offered protection from southern winds; together they offered the best natural anchorages in the whole of Sicily, and arguably the Greek west. The Fountain of Arethusa on Ortygia provided an endless supply of water. The Corinthians soon built a ramp to connect Ortygia to Sicily proper, and settled there too. At Gela, on the other hand, no such ideal harbours were to be found and did not seem to matter; the settlers occupied a ridge running close to the shore and hauled their ships up on the sandy beach. What there was was the water of the river debouching here into the ocean suitable for consumption and irrigation, and vast acres of land for agriculture and the raising of horses.

The urban shape, character and early history of these settlements is not well documented. The literary sources are quiet and the archaeological record is very fragmentary; in most instances subsequent construction on top of early levels has effectively destroyed early buildings; building materials were perishable and perished. It is plain, however, that the colonists brought their own religions with them. At Syracuse, the two temples of the sixth century BC are dedicated to Olympian Zeus and to Apollo. Athena was accommodated in the early fifth century BC in a hexastyle Doric building, which nowadays forms the core of the Cathedral: of this temple, the northern stylobate and colonnade, now built into a wall, are still visible, and the cella walls were punctured to create the aisles of the church. An inscription of the fifth century BC from Selinus in western Sicily, associated with the vast unfinished Temple G, perhaps gives the flavour of Greek religious life in Sicily most clearly: a dedication to Apollo, it records gratitude to 'Zeus, Phobos, Herakles, Poseidon, and the Tyndaridae, Athena, Malophoros, Pasikrateia, and other gods, particularly Zeus'. There are notable absentees from the Greek pantheon here, but this is emphatic epigraphic evidence: repetitive, to be sure, and to that extent, naive, but authentic. Since monumental sanctuaries were built for the Olympians from the sixth century on, it is obvious that they came with the original founders and were housed initially in structures built of primitive and impermanent materials.

Early Buildings

Greek cults, then, came with the original settlers to the West. Yet there is no reason, necessarily, to suppose that stoneworking skills also came with craftsmen from Greece. It may have been so, but, equally, artisans in Magna Graecia could as probably have learnt from centres of experimentation and development such as the Cyclades and Samos, as from itinerant or emigré masons. However that may be, temples began to be built of local limestone from the mid-sixth century onward, originally with monolithic columns (e.g. Apollo and Zeus at Syracuse); architects invariably rang the changes on the conservative vocabulary of Doric temple building in Greece and introduced new elements (e.g., most obviously, the double colonnade at front). Stonebuilt treasuries, altars and other cultic buildings also came to the fore. Some of these buildings were expensively decorated with carved and painted metopes which show a range of myth and didactic power unrivalled anywhere in the Greek world. Selinus, for example, boasted at least half a dozen temples of the Archaic period (*c.* 600 BC–*c.* 480 BC), some of which were embellished with such metopes, now to be seen in the Museo Archeologico in Palermo: among mythological scenes, Europa and the Bull, for example, is depicted. The metopes from the so-called Treasury in the sanctuary of Hera at the Foce del Sele (see Chapter 4) illustrate heroic cycles in which some of the incidents are not surely identifiable (though speculation proliferates) and scenes unknown elsewhere in the Greek world appear. In fact, so rich is the Greek West in the production and variety of carved architectural metopes of the sixth century that some commentators have proposed that it is in Magna Graecia that temple builders first introduced the idea.

This theory is difficult to resist. In Greece, although painted terracotta metopes occur as early as *c.* 630 BC, the earliest stone carved metopes are those recovered from the foundations of the Treasury of the Sikyonians at Delphi – unless the sculpted block found at Mycenae and known as the 'Woman at the Window' is to be thought of as a metope. If quantity and variety of execution and content count for anything, then Magna Graecia has a good claim to be considered the birthplace of the sculpted stone Doric metope.

Early Neighbours

The Greek masons, sculptors, architects, potters, painters and other craftsmen who worked in Magna Graecia in the sixth century BC possessed tools and technological knowhow far in advance of those used by the people with whom they came in touch. In Sicily, the Greeks came into contact with Sicels in the east and Sicans in the west; and the long process of possession and dispossession, and of cultural exchange at every level – political, social, economic, artistic – began. No such exchange, however, was in the air with regard to the other foreigners the Greeks found in the west of the island, the Carthaginians. By contrast, here was direct antagonism and competition, unresolved until the great battle won by Theron of Acragas with his ally Gelon of Syracuse at Himera in 480 BC. This was a conflict as meaningful for the Greeks in the West as that in the same year at Salamis was for Greeks in Greece.

In South Italy, the indigenous tribes are not easy to disentangle either chronologically or geographically, though broad outlines are visible. The literary sources speak of the Ausones as early settlers throughout the south; there are also Oenotri, and unnamed dwellers in the central hills from whom the Lucani are said to be descended, and tribes of Illyrian, i.e. Balkan, origin along the southeast coast and in the interior behind. Tribes of Etruscan origin had also pressed southward in the interior forming a chain of settlements in Campania just inland from the coast, e.g. at Capua, Nola and Pontecagnano. Continuing southward, they had occupied the Vallo di Diano, where they flourished from the ninth to the fifth centuries BC astride the commercial north-south and east-west crossroads. When Greek settlers arrived, the process of acculturation began. The paucity of archaeological evidence for Greek settlements in the east suggests that the Illyrian tribes there were not disposed to welcome the newcomers. Elsewhere, contacts were established, and exchanges thrived. With respect to cults, for example, it seems that the two divinities from the Greek pantheon which appealed most to local inhabitants were Demeter and Aphrodite. Thus, indigenous tribes of Central Italy, such as the Paelignians, even joined the worship of the two goddesses under the care of a single female priesthood, the *sacerdotes Cereris et Veneris*.

Sybaris

Among the more well-known, if not notorious, Greek colonial foundations was that at Sybaris. The ancient sources speak of the wealth of the city in extravagant terms, while the citizens were known far and wide for their idleness and for the luxuriousness of their living – hence, the modern word for such a lifestyle: sybaritic. Wine was piped directly into the city from the vineyards, according to Athenaeus, while no roosters were allowed by law within the city walls for fear of waking people too early. This colony was founded *c.* 720 BC by exiles from Achaea and Troizen. Their arrival was not peaceful. Indigenous settlements (peopled by the Oenotri) in the nearby hinterland such as that at Francavilla Maritima came to a sudden end: the populations, we may suppose, were either destroyed or enslaved. At Francavilla, the Greeks showed no restraint; to mark their conquest, they built a sanctuary of Athena on top of the ruined Oenotrian village.

Sybaris grew rapidly, profiting from the rich open plain in which she stood, and which had made the area a focus for population for centuries. Other foreigners were welcomed into the citizenship, according to Diodoros, while Strabo reckoned that at the height of her power Sybaris controlled no less than 25 towns. Excavation at Amendolara, to the north of the site of Sybaris, has revealed traces of a township which flourished at exactly the time that Sybaris did (i.e. *c.* 720–*c.* 510 BC), and which doubtless fell under the politcal sway of Sybaris. The close relationship between Sybaris and Miletus, one of the principal Greek cities on the coast of Asia Minor, became well known: Herodotos tells us that when Sybaris was sacked by Croton at the end of the sixth century, the Milesians tore their hair as an expression of grief. The Mileto-Sybaris connection certainly spelt trade, and provided a conduit for goods from Miletus into the west. Miletus was herself an emporium of great renown receiving goods and influences from Asia Minor (among other places) and sending secondary settlements from Miletus up into the Black Sea; accordingly, it is tempting to imagine that attitudes of spendthrift extravagance may have arrived in Sybaris from Sardis, recognized centre (at any rate in the Greek mind) of wealth, refined excess, and lavish living in the sixth century BC. Trade from the east, and fertile agricultural land aplenty, were then the two sources of Sybaris' amazing wealth.

Like many other colonies in Magna Graecia, Sybaris participated in a second wave of colonization some 100 years after her own foundation. Sicilian Naxos sent some of her people to found Leontinoi: Acragas was founded from Gela – and from Rhodes again, original participant in the foundation of Gela – early in the sixth century. The creation of these new colonies probably implies the success of the original foundations, and perhaps implies tensions between tribal groups within a city. It certainly points to population growth, and in some cases (e.g. Naxos) concomitant land shortage. In some instances, commercial motives may also have come into play: access to sources of metals was always a powerful incentive.

Elements of the population of Sybaris were sent to new foundations at a number of places, prominent among which are Laos and Poseidonia. Herodotos remarks that survivors of the sack of Sybaris by Croton at the end of the sixth century found refuge at Laos. A precious comment of Aristotle informs us that the Achaeans and Troizenians, the original settlers of Sybaris, had a nasty quarrel as a result of which the Troizenians were driven out of the city. They fled north and founded Poseidonia.

CHAPTER TWO

POSEIDONIA:
THE SIXTH-CENTURY CITY

Early Settlers

When the Troizenians, exiles for a second time, arrived to settle Poseidonia, they found a plain ripe for agricultural development with ample water and forested mountains behind. They would have had little reason to know of or distrust the calcifying properties of springs near where the temples were to be or those of the Capodifiume, the springs from which the water which formed the River Salso emerged, at the foot of the hills behind the plain. There is no evidence of dwellings from the site of the city or of tombs nearby to suggest that the newcomers met and displaced an original indigenous settlement; though we should be alert to arguments from silence when the record is so incomplete.

A Palaeolithic presence (a hunting camp?) is attested by flint implements found close to the basilica, while Neolithic peoples were active near where the Temple of Athena was to be and in the zone between the temple and the Porta Aurea (the north gate). A large cemetery of the second millennium BC (perhaps from *c.* 1800 BC) was found during World War II by American troops preparing an airstrip about one mile (1.6 km) north of the classical city in the *località* known as Gaudo: the graves were cut in a limestone shelf, each grave consisting of an antechamber like a well, and a chamber or chambers; burials were multiple, and grave goods included arrowheads, daggers and tools of flint, copper daggers (rarely) and handmade pottery. This cemetery proves the existence of a Bronze Age village of considerable size in the vicinity. Similar materials have been found in Campania to the north, and at Eboli, a few miles north of Paestum, and together these concentrations attest the arrival of new peoples in Campania and on the Sele plain with new burial customs, and a knowledge of the technology of metals.

Close to the south wall of the city, the remains of a Late Bronze Age dwelling have come to light; and the discovery here of a pair of Mycenaean sherds shows contact, however indirect, with the wider Mediterranean world. Hints of other Late Bronze Age structures have come from the new excavations in the *località* Santa Venera, again close to the south wall, and Strabo, the first century BC/AD scholar and geographer had been told of a tradition of pre-Greek settlement. According to Strabo's source, it was the Thessalian hero Jason, with his colleagues the Argonauts, fresh from their adventures in retrieving the golden fleece but blown off course on their return to Greece, who landed here. This version of the legend may be taken to reflect either a Thessalian origin for the first Greek settlers – in contrast to the generally accepted Sybarite origin – or the presence of foreign mariners here, themselves Greek, before the historical Greek settlement. Of the Early Iron Age at Paestum, we are ill-informed; c. 800 BC a group of farmers settled close to the Capodifiume on the slopes of the hills of Capaccio behind the city, where characteristically Villanovan biconical urns have been found, and cremation burial was practised. In the second half of the seventh century groups of settlers appeared at two sites, Rovine di Palma and Tempalta, some 6–9 miles (10–15 km) northeast of where the new city was to be. Their pottery, for the most part, shows connections with the material culture of Pontecagnano north of the Sele; given the size of this great Etruscan urban complex, this should not surprise. However, other elements from the tombs at Tempalta – bowls and pitchers, objects of bronze and amber – show more local, indigenous, Oenotrian typologies. More evidence will doubtless come to light of indigenous, Etruscan-influenced penetration south of the Sele in the northeast corner of the plain, astride the valley routes leading south. The denizens of these sites, settled on the eve of the arrival of the Greeks, must have viewed the newcomers with some interest. Beyond these two sites, however, there is nothing yet, except scraps of seventh-century pottery excavated on the site of the city itself, to suggest that the plain where the Greeks were to build their city was inhabited.

Strabo says that when the colonists arrived, they settled first on the shore, and that it was a second wave of colonists who inhabited the site known as Poseidonia. Argument continues as to where Strabo's first settlement is to be located. Some argue the claims of the mouth of the river Sele, surely a convenient landing place and close to where the great sanctuary of Hera was soon to be built. Others suggest that the peninsula of Agropoli is topographically more probable and point to the existence of a cult of Poseidon himself at Agropoli as testified to by Lycophron (*Alexandra* 722). Indeed, recent excavations in the area of the so called Saracen castle on the hilltop at Agropoli have produced much sixth-century Greek material which included fragments of architectural terracottas, similar to those which decorated the roof of the oldest of the temples at Poseidonia, the basilica. However that may be, Strabo is no help – nor is any other literary source for that matter – in assessing the date of the arrival of the Greeks. For this, we turn to the archaeological record. The oldest Greek pottery emerging from the tombs of the colonists to the north and northeast of the city is of the end of the Early Corinthian style (*c.* 625–*c.* 600 BC in general terms), from which we may conclude that Greeks settled here *c.* 600 BC. Similarly, the oldest materials from the excavations at the Heraion at Foce del Sele date

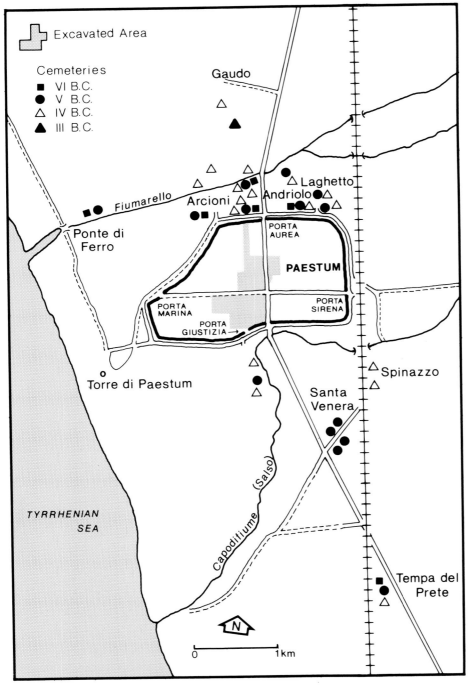

8 Plan of Paestum and immediate environs showing city gates, cemeteries, and streams flowing either side of the city. The Tomb of the Diver was found in the Tempa del Prete to the south, while Lucanian painted tombs have come to light on all sides (except towards the sea).

to *c.* 600 BC. The establishment of the sanctuary at Foce del Sele, immediately opposite the Etruscan settlement on the other side the Sele at Pontecagnano, defined the northward extent of the new city's territory, and invoked the protection of the goddess, while the city itself was located close to the other source of water, the springs of the Capodifiume, and dominated the southern half of the plain. Twin contemporaneous settlements perhaps reflect Strabo's two phases of arrival; could the sources on which Strabo drew have misunderstood a record of two locations of settlement for two phases of arrival?

Geology

The site chosen for the layout of the city was a shelf of calcareous limestone, rising somewhat above the level of the plain. Its trapezoidal shape dictated the line of the city walls which were to run for *c.* 3 miles (4.8 km) and include *c.* 240 acres (96 ha). The shelf (or crust or plate or terrace) of calcareous limestone, conventionally referred to as travertine, is just one of a series which go to form the stratigraphic profile of the site. Archaeologically, these travertine shelves are both troublesome and helpful: troublesome in the sense that they are difficult to dig through, and helpful in that they seal deposits firmly. They are formed by the precipitation of calcium carbonate from spring waters in more or less stagnant water. The depth of the water and the distance from the spring control the types of deposit which result from the precipitation, and these range from calcareous muds to hard, tough travertine.

In the region of Paestum it is the waters of the Capodifiume supercharged with calcium carbonate which are responsible for the formation of the crusts. These crusts took shape as large horizontal sheets in marshes or shallow lakes and testify that at the moment of their formation, the area was inundated and without drainage schemes. When drainage systems were introduced, or spring waters took a different course, the upper surfaces of the crusts received a secondary cementation and became impermeable: this impermeability of the crusts was to be a matter of concern for builders coping with drainage problems.

The best known and most easily recognized of these crusts is the so-called medieval *crosta* (X), found far and wide at Paestum; this travertine plate sits on top of medieval material of the thirteenth century AD. The recent excavations in the *località* Santa Venera have revealed three other chronologically distinct crusts (I, III and V); the earliest Greek buildings were founded on one of these (V), and all four are interspersed with soil strata. These soil strata have recently been shown to include volcanic debris from Vesuvius, so that in general terms the stratigraphy of the site presents an alternation of travertine crusts (I, III, V, X) and pumiceous volcanic strata (II, IV, VIa, VII) interspersed with strata demonstrating human activity of one kind and

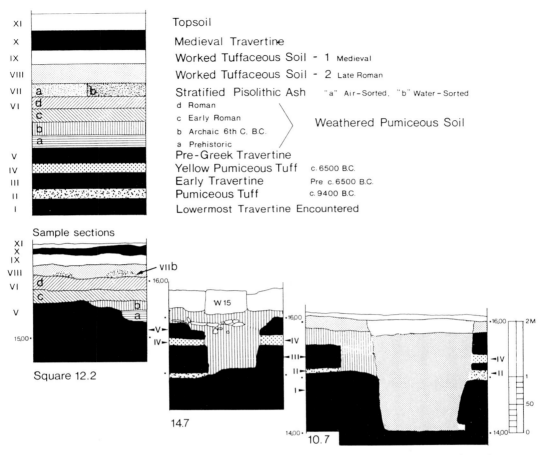

XI	Topsoil
X	Medieval Travertine
IX	Worked Tuffaceous Soil - 1 Medieval
VIII	Worked Tuffaceous Soil - 2 Late Roman
VII	Stratified Pisolithic Ash "a" Air–Sorted, "b" Water–Sorted
VI	d Roman
	c Early Roman
	b Archaic 6th C. B.C. Weathered Pumiceous Soil
	a Prehistoric
V	Pre-Greek Travertine
IV	Yellow Pumiceous Tuff c. 6500 B.C.
III	Early Travertine Pre c. 6500 B.C.
II	Pumiceous Tuff c. 9400 B.C.
I	Lowermost Travertine Encountered

Sample sections

Square 12.2

14.7

10.7

9 Sanctuary in the località *Santa Venera, diagram of strata. A composite drawing (top left) and sections through three excavated squares show the various chronologically distinct travertine crusts (I, III, V, X) formed by the precipitation of calcium carbonate from springwaters. These rock crusts are interspersed with soil strata larded with deposits of datable volcanic debris (II, IV VIa, VII) which enable a tentative chronology to be assigned to the formation of the crusts. With this kind of evidence, environmental archaeologists may be able to reconstruct the history of the ancient landscape around the city.*

10 Sanctuary in the località *Santa Venera. Channel cut in the crusts outside the east wall of the Rectangular Hall (to the left), showing travertine crusts V (upper) and III (lower) and soil stratum (IV) between the two.*

another. Put another way, there were periods when conditions at Paestum were swampy and crusts formed; other periods when volcanic discharges were deposited; and yet other periods of adequate drainage, healthy conditions, and human activity.

The existence of strata comprising volcanic matter provides unexpected and important chronological markers. Coordinated with ceramic evidence, they yield the following chronology: the oldest crust of which we know (I) formed before *c.* 9400 BC, stratum III before *c.* 6500 BC, and stratum V before *c.* 1500 BC. The recognition of these volcanic deposits takes the history of the site back to the tenth millennium BC. It also affords the possibility of correlations over large distances in the wide surround of Vesuvius with obvious implications for the reconstruction of the ancient landscape at various moments in antiquity.

The Harbour

A first necessity for the Greeks settling at Poseidonia was a place to put their ships. There is no obvious anchorage today near the city; on the other hand, the coastline has changed drastically since antiquity. Debate has therefore raged as to whether the newcomers beached their ships or found a suitable anchorage nearby.

Some have taken the view that the harbour was located at or near the mouth of the river Sele, close to the famous Heraion. Given the fact that the Sele is the only sizeable river mouth along the coast between Agropoli and Salerno, it is hardly to be doubted that boats will have landed there, and some trade will have ensued; but the location is a long way (*c.* 5.5 miles (8.5 km)) from the city and no harbour installations have been found. Another candidate is Agropoli, with its promontory offering anchorage and shelter both on the north and on the south in a topographical configuration much favoured by Greek explorers; yet here again no archaeological evidence has yet come to light, and here again, the site is a fair distance away (*c.* 5 miles (8 km)).

The existence of a harbour to the west and northwest of the Porta Marina, right at Poseidonia, in a lagoonal zone, has also been proposed; and this theory continues to attract support. Recent scientific exploration has, however, shown that though there was a lagoon there in the early second millennium BC, it would have been too shallow to accommodate shipping, and that in the Greek period, the area, no longer lagoonal, was separated from the open sea by a dune ridge – through which drainage channels were cut – and was marshy and quiescent. The dune ridge formed a substantial coastal barrier some 400 metres at its closest point from the city walls; and this dune ridge has recently yielded, near Ponte di Ferro, some 850 metres northwest of the city walls, Greek burials of the sixth century BC. It seems then that the ancient topography and environment made no provision for a natural harbour; furthermore, by the rapid formation of marshy zones richly fed by springwaters with calcifying properties, it also discouraged the construction of an artificial anchorage close to what was to be the Porta Marina. Evidently, the Troizenian colonists contented themselves, like their counterparts at Gela in Sicily, with hauling up their ships on the beach which here must have been located on the seaward side of the dune ridge. The short stretch of low flat beach directly in front of, and not less than some 400 metres distant from, the travertine shelf on which they were to lay out their new city, would have had appeal enough.

The Town Plan

It is difficult to give exact dates to the city walls. It is, however, obvious that they were built in phases, that they have been heavily restored, and that they follow the edge of the travertine shelf on which they sit. It is equally obvious that, whatever their date of construction, walls would have been planned from the first, and that their four gates were aligned with the points of the compass.

Within the walls two fixed points of the sixth century are the basilica close to the Porta Giustizia at the south, and the Temple of Athena close to the Port Aurea at the north. It is noticeable that they are both aligned in similar fashion and that this alignment is parallel to a hypothetical line joining the Porta Giustizia to the Porta Aurea. The original city plan does not then, at a glance, *seem* to be reflected in the ancient roads, streets and houses visible at Paestum today; these are all of Roman date (or were in use in the Roman period) and follow a different orientation. Either, then, the Romans, or conceivably the Lucanians before them, entirely revamped the gridplan of the city when they arrived, or the sixth-century temples (and then the fifth-century Temple of Hera II also) reflect an architectural alignment attuned to cultic needs which coexisted with alignments drawn on different axes for secular structures and zones. The latter theory, without parallel in Greek town planning and therefore somewhat unlikely, implies that the orientation of the temples, though linked to that of the notional alignment between the north and south gates, tells little about the layout of the Greek city. There are two further complicating factors. The first is that a small archaic temple, recently discovered beneath the imperial *curia* and *macellum* on the south side of the Roman Forum, does *not* follow the alignment of the larger upstanding Greek temples, but is aligned on the same axis as the visible road system. A second is that the shops at the west end of the Forum, the installation of which seems to have taken place contemporaneously with the arrangement of the Forum space, i.e. shortly after 273 BC, appear to be founded on part of the N-S roadway and indeed to curtail it; accordingly, the roadway appears to be assignable to a pre-Roman period. This problem has been with us for fifty years since first articulated by Maiuri: we are getting more information from the work of Greco and Theodorescu in the central zones of the city now, but even more is needed.

Sixth-century Greek urban planning tended to arrange streets and houses in gridlike blocks, a tradition codified by Hippodamos of Miletus, and such is the case at nearby Metapontum, planned at about the same time as Poseidonia. Aerial photography reveals such a regular arrangement at Paestum, of the Roman period, thoughout the area within the walls; but we are hampered by the fact that much of this area is privately owned and has not been systematically explored. It is reasonable, however, to suppose an original plan which called for parallel streets at right angles to one another, as at Metapontum, forming long and narrow blocks of houses. Separate areas accommodated public buildings, and are exemplified by the zones reserved for the sanctuaries of Hera and Athena. Such a layout would have been entirely in accord with theories of town planning in the Greek West.

Cemeteries

Dwellings of the dead have been found to the north of the city in the *contrade* of Laghetto and Arcioni and by the Ponte di Ferro. Burials in the cemeteries of Laghetto and Arcioni were simple: corpses were interred in graves cut in the rock and covered by tiles, or occasionally in wooden or tilemade coffins. Infants were buried in *amphorae* (storage jars) and the quantity of these inhumations tells its own tale: infant mortality rates were high. Grave goods are as simple as the graves: only an occasional flash of luxury is provided by the Corinthian *aryballoi* (for perfume or oil) of the first half of the century or by East Greek *balsamaria* (similar purpose) of the second. Attic black figure pottery which displaced Corinthian throughout the Greek world by the middle of the century, is hard to find, though *lekythoi* (again flasks for oil) appear from time to time, and a very few cups. Even the prolific 'Ionic' cups are a rarity. Overall, the picture is of a struggling, homogeneous community undivided by social distinctions.

At Ponte di Ferro, the picture is even balder. Here graves are dug in the sand, and sometimes are covered by bizarrely shaped tiles, so misshapen that they could only have been rejects, i.e. wasters. The graves are positioned huggermugger, often violate other graves, and the few that have grave goods are content with only local imitations of imported pottery. The extreme poverty of this graveyard, and its location by the sea, allows the conjecture that it may have been for slaves who perhaps were involved with the loading and unloading of ships.

The Underground Shrine

Perhaps the most intriguing structure of the sixth-century city, itself perhaps a kind of tomb, is the so-called Underground Shrine. Found by Pellegrino

11 Shrine and temenos wall from southwest. Note the double roofing system, a lower of stone and an upper of huge terracotta tiles, and absence of doorway.

The Underground Shrine

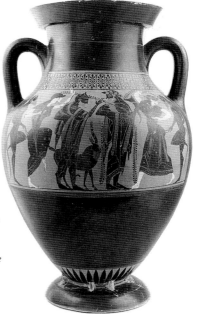

12, 13 (above) Bronze hydria of the late sixth century BC. One of eight bronze vessels (six hydriai and two amphorae) found by Pellegrino Sestieri in 1954 still containing the sticky substance (honey?) with which they were filled in antiquity. (right) Attic black-figure amphora of c. 510 BC from the Shrine. The panel shows Dionysos, Hermes and followers; the other side depicts the reception of Herakles by the Olympian gods, an apotheosis. Note the lead clamps with which the foot was reattached to the body after being damaged in antiquity.

Sestieri in 1954 in the area between the later Roman Forum and the Temple of Athena, it was entirely covered by earth, in tumulus fashion and hence invisible. Roughly rectangular in shape, it was built of limestone ashlars and, oddly, was equipped with two gabled roofs: the lower with stone roofing tiles, and a second, on top, with terracotta tiles. Three sides of the edifice were partially encased in the travertine crust, cut to take the building, while the fourth, the eastern, was unencumbered. There are no doors, windows or any openings so that the structure was, so to speak, sealed from the exterior; it is more reminiscent of tombs built within tumuli such as those which decorated the landscapes of Phrygia and Lydia at Gordion and Sardis.

The excavators gained entrance through the roof and found a curious agglomeration of objects inside. Arranged along the walls were six *hydriai* (water jars) and two *amphorae* of bronze; three of the *hydriai* decorated with female heads at the foot of the vertical handle seem to be of Laconian provenance, while another which sports a vertical handle in the form of a lion is the product of a successful and technologically advanced studio, perhaps here in the Greek West. These vessels were brimful with a brown sticky substance like molasses ('honey' is the term generally used) at the time of their discovery. Also in the chamber was a single Athenian black-figure *amphora* with the front panel depicting the apotheosis of Herakles, that on the reverse, a Dionysiac scene: this *amphora* had been repaired before being placed in the chamber, and the fact that a repaired pot was judged worthy of inclusion suggests that it had a special significance – the heroic apotheosis? In the middle of the room were five big iron spits laid out on two travertine blocks; fragments of leather and textiles were also found. The dates attributable to the bronzes and to the Athenian *amphora* show that this complex was built and closed sometime *c.* 510–500 BC. Later, perhaps sometime in the late fourth or early third century (and if so, after the arrival of the Romans) it was surrounded by a protective precinct wall emphasizing the religious character of the building.

Many theories have been advanced to explain this complex. First, that it was a place of worship of an underground cult, that of Hera = Kore, daughter of Demeter, Queen of the Underworld. Second, that it was sacred to the Nymphs – this on the basis of a graffito scratched on a Greek vase found near the building and saying 'I am sacred to the Nymph'. Third, that the building was the site of marriage vows and rites for young women – interpreting the Nymph of the graffito generically. Fourth, and more plausibly, that the monument was the cenotaph, i.e. empty tomb, of the founder of Sybaris, heroized after death, as all founding fathers were, and worshipped in a cult – this on the grounds of the chronology of the structure and the known departure of the Sybarites from Sybaris *c.* 510 BC after their defeat at the hands of the Crotoniates. Though the literary sources do not mention Poseidonia as a place of refuge for the Sybarites, and do mention

14 Sixth-century silver coin of Poseidonia. Poseidon strides to the right while brandishing his trident (awkwardly, held in the right hand but visible beyond his head to allow the face to be seen). The letters POS stand to the left. This coin may reflect a now lost statue of the god.

Laos and Skidros (Herodotos), it is highly likely that some Sybarites would have come to Poseidonia, and been welcome. Fifth, a new interpretation has been given to the building on the basis of recent excavations and the identification of much of the zone between the Temple of Athena and the Roman Forum as the political heart of the Greek city. The underground building marks the western edge of the Agora, the geographical focus of the democratic city, and its location is therefore significant; it was indeed a cenotaph and a Heroon, but a Heroon of an important political figure to whom an important political cult was dedicated, and not that of a mythological founder. Yet one wonders whether convention would allow anyone at all to be buried, or remembered, within the city's walls. The cenotaph of a mythological person is one thing, that of a person who had actually lived quite another. Sixth, and finally, it has recently been suggested that the structure and its contents were indeed an offering to Hera = Kore, and that the cult was chthonic, at any rate in part. That the epithet 'The Nymph' was sometimes attached to Hera explains the graffito, and it is suggested that this underground complex was a gift of the Sybarites after the destruction of their city in an attempt to assuage a Hera angered at their conduct, as Athenaeus, the prolific writer of the second/third centuries AD records.

Trade and Coinage

Contact with the outside world is shown not only by the arrival of Sybarites towards the end of the century, but obviously by the presence of foreign imports, e.g. Corinthian pottery, from the very beginning. Athenian pottery, 'Ionic' cups, and East Greek *balsamaria* (flasks for perfume or oil) of which a notable example comes in the form of a sandalled foot (!) have come to light, and objects of Egyptian faience which made their way to the West through the Greek emporion at Naukratis in the Egyptian delta. Transport *amphorae* of types associated with Corinth, Chios and Samos also tell of the import of oil and wine from the Greek East. The advent of coinage too bespeaks links with others. Around the middle of the century Poseidonia began to strike her own coins. This was a silver coinage, and the coins at the start were incuse, i.e. an image was stamped in relief on one side of the coin and produced a concave impression on the other. For her emblem Poseidonia chose, naturally enough, Poseidon who appears striding and brandishing a trident; one wonders whether the emblem might reflect the cult statue of Poseidon itself. The use of the incuse technique shows close contact with other colonies founded originally from Achaea, i.e., Sybaris, Metapontum, Caulonia, and Croton. The coinage was evidently usable by other Greeks, and would doubtless have had a currency among the Ionian Greeks from Phocaea in Asia Minor who settled at Velia shortly after the middle of the century: Velia is close to Poseidonia to the south, and the colony could only have been established with the agreement of Poseidonia, and though she struck her own coinage would also have made use of the coinage of Poseidonia. Towards the end of the century, the city abandoned the incuse technique for the production of coins, and the bull of Sybaris appears on the reverse of the new coinage: this seems to support the idea that refugees from Sybaris came to Poseidonia shortly after the disastrous events of *c.* 510 BC.

Grave goods from the necropoleis at Laghetto, Arcioni and Ponte di Ferro give a picture of a new colonial society not endowed with any great wealth. Yet the striking of her own coinage from about the middle years of the century, and the ambitious building programme (see next chapter) which began at about the same time show that something was afoot. Votive materials from sanctuaries provide further information.

Votives

The offerings made by devotees to favoured divinities consist for the most part of terracotta figurines. The sanctuaries of Poseidonia have yielded thousands of these images which, though often recovered from pits which had suffered reuse and therefore chronological contamination, are nevertheless easily datable on the grounds of style and type. Similar figurines were dedicated to divinities throughout Magna Graecia, while some are easily recognizable as foreign types (e.g. from Corinth or Rhodes); examples of foreign types were both imported wholesale, and fabricated from imported moulds with handmade additions. Popular sixth-century types in Poseidonia included the enthroned female type without attributes or holding a child (= Hera Kourotrophos) or with a small horse held to the breast (= Hera Hippia) or holding a pomegranate; other less favoured but informative types include a standing female figure brandishing a spear (= Hera Hoplosmia) and a standing nude female (= Aphrodite/Astarte). These figures underscored

15 (left) Terracotta figurine of Hera Kourotrophos, sixth century BC. Such figurines were votive offerings to the goddess in her aspect as the nurturer, and have been found in great numbers both in the city sanctuaries and at the Heraion at Foce del Sele. Flattened lower body and painted surfaces are characteristic.

16 (above) Terracotta figurine of Hera Hoplosmia, sixth century BC. Another votive type represents another aspect of the goddess Hera. In warlike posture, she is here the defiant protector of the city.

the centrality of women in cultic life in the sixth century, with obvious emphasis on the mysteries of sexuality and reproduction, and provide firm evidence for a thriving artistic and religious life in the new colony.

Ancient authors tell us nothing about the growth and development of the city or about its life and times. An inscribed bronze tablet, however, written in archaic Greek and found at Olympia, lifts the curtain for a moment. The tablet reads: 'The Sybarites and their allies and the Serdaioi are yoked together in terms of true and guileless friendship for ever, the guarantors are Zeus, Apollo and the other gods, and the city of Poseidonia.' So, Poseidonia became the real arbiter, with some pretty impressive support, between Sybaris and the Serdaioi (the location of which is still unknown, though the obvious association with Sardinia has been mooted); and this bronze tablet allows us a glimpse of Poseidonia as an important city-state playing a key role in the political life of the Greek West. The literary sources may be silent: the monumental architecture, to which we now turn, is not.

17 Temple of Hera I. The oldest temple at Poseidonia, built in the middle years of the sixth century BC. View of the west façade, the back of the building, from the southwest with the Temple of Hera II beyond. Note the pronounced entasis *(cigarlike swelling) of the columns.*

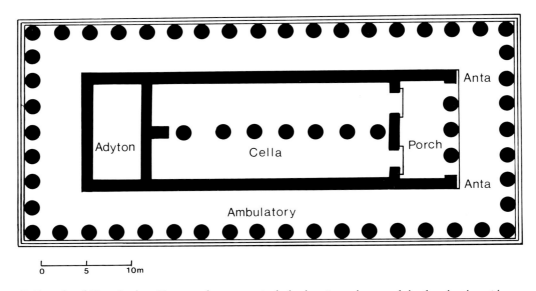

18 Temple of Hera I, plan. Noteworthy aspects include the nine columns of the façade, the wide ambulatory, the three columns of the porch, and the single row of columns in the cella.

CHAPTER THREE

THE SIXTH-CENTURY TEMPLES

The Basilica (Temple of Hera I)

Sometime about the middle of the sixth century work began on the imposing building known erroneously as the basilica, in the large sacred area in the southern part of the city. In the organization of the townplan this zone was earmarked for religious purposes and the limits of the area had been fixed by sandstone boundary markers (*horoi*). The term basilica is a misnomer employed by scholars of the eighteenth century who could not reconcile with temple architecture an uneven number of columns at the front, and back, the apparent absence of pediments, and an interior dividing colonnade; they therefore saw the building as a civil administrative structure. The temple was built to a highly imaginative plan, with a central axial colonnade in the *cella*, three columns in the porch (which dictated the number of columns on the façade), much descriptive detail and evidence of Achaean architectural influence. It faced east and measures *c.* 24.5 × 54.3 m. There is much debate about when the temple was built, and proponents have suggested dates as early as the 570s or as late as the 520s. A major difficulty is the apparent divergence between the plan, which seems eccentric and early, and the more conventional style of the architectural terracottas.

Nine columns on the façade and eighteen on the flank immediately mark the building out as exceptional. The architect has started with the requirements of a single row of columns in the interior either as a deliberately retrospective glance at earlier temple construction, or as a means of providing equal space for two cult statues and two cults or a double cult (Zeus and Hera are the obvious candidates; terracotta votives showing the *hierogamia*, the sacred marriage, depict the two enthroned together) or as both. The preservation of the axial line of the row of columns of the *cella* required three columns (not the usual two) in the porch, a bold stroke, and this in turn required nine on the façade. Thus the planner(s) bisected not only the *cella*, but also the porch and the façade at once. They also called for the dimensions of the cella columns to be the same as those of the exterior, a most unusual and perhaps even unique specification, since cella columns are regularly smaller than those of the peristyle. An *adyton*, to safeguard the temple's goods, behind the *cella* balanced the porch at front; this space had originally been a back porch, an *opisthodomos*. It is worth remarking that in spite of the probability of a double cult, and the innovative plan which this demanded, some commentators continue to regard the plan as provincial and passé; this on account of the single central row of columns in the cella, an echo of earlier arrangements as, for example, at seventh-century Thermon in Greece.

The columns display the *entasis* characteristic of the early Doric Order, i.e. the midpart of the column swells out in cigarlike shape while the upper tapers towards the join with the capital. *Entasis* was thought necessary to correct an optical illusion: if the contour lines of the column shaft were absolutely straight, though inclining inward as they tapered up, the shaft would have appeared as concave. The degree of *entasis* is normally taken as an index of date (the more visible the *entasis*, the earlier the date) and the pronounced swelling of these columns proclaim their early, archaic date. The necks of the capitals, directly above the join with the column shaft, are decorated in flamboyant style with *anthemion* collars, i.e. in this instance a decoration of stylized tongue-like leaves. At the back of the building some capitals received a second ornamental register circling the *echinus* itself immediately above the collar of tongue-like leaves; lotus flowers, rosettes,

---

Colour plates I–VI

I *Via Sacra* (cardo maximus), *from the south. The cobbled main north-south thoroughfare of the city with the remnants of the* temenos (precinct) *wall of the sanctuary to the right, and the temples of Hera beyond.*

II *Temple of Hera I, sometimes erroneously still called the basilica, from the east. The oldest of the three Greek temples at Poseidonia, this building is distinctive both for its unusual plan and for details of the elevation.*

III *Temple of Hera II, from the west. Built a hundred years later than the Temple of Hera I, to the south, the temple is both more conspicuous for its bulk, and less imaginative in its plan than its predecessor.*

IV *Temple of Hera II, interior, showing ambulatory with peristyle columns to the left, lowest courses of masonry of* cella *wall to the right with the two storeys of columns of the inside of the* cella *beyond.*

V *Temple of Athena, from the northwest. Daring innovations mark this structure as the brainchild of a specially gifted architect. This is the first building, of which we know, to use both Doric and Ionic columns; in so doing, it precedes by half a century the same usage employed in the Parthenon at Athens.*

VI *Temple of Athena, interior, from the east, showing blocks of lowest courses of porch and* cella *walls, and much eroded bases for the Ionic columns of the porch; the north peristyle is seen to the right, and interior of the back elevation to the left.*

I

II III

IV

V VI

tendrils, palmettes and petals are among motifs employed. These motifs have been ambitiously interpreted by some scholars as evidence of masons competing with one another, and identifying their work by particular designs. Too distant from the eye to be sculpturally visible, these details would have provided colourful accents when picked out, as they originally were, with paint. The *echinus* of the capital (the lower of the two members) has the squashed convex profile typical of archaic architecture; here again, the degree of convexity of the profile is taken as a chronological index, the more sagging the profile, the earlier the date. The upper of the two members of the capital, the *abacus*, is the normal flat rectangular block.

Above the capitals the architrave is separated from the frieze course, of which only the backers are preserved, by a string course of sandstone; this too was originally decorated with stylized tongue-like leaves, and by the warmth of its natural colour alone injected a lively visual note into the superstructure. The backing blocks of the frieze course preserve in their ends the large U-shaped cuttings used for lifting the blocks into place with ropes: not a single triglyph or metope of the frieze itself has, however, been preserved. The carved stone metope depicting Europa and the Bull, found in the *località* Santa Venera some 475 metres away, and now in the Naples Museum, has been thought of as originally belonging to one of the major temples; but its fragmentary condition and poor state of preservation render conjecture about the original size of the metope difficult, and not a single other carved metope has been found in, or in the vicinity of, the city. It seems that the metopes of the basilica were undecorated or, possibly, painted. Nothing remains *in situ* above the frieze course, but many fragments of the painted architectural terracottas which decorated the eaves of the roof have been found. Against a brightly painted background of registers of palmettes, tongue patterns, swastikas and quatrefoils, painted gutter spouts in the form of lionheads project. On top of the eaves stands a series of antefixes in the shape of huge palmettes which run along the flank of the building. The excavations unearthed evidence of another series of architectural terracottas of the fourth century BC which show, unsurprisingly, that the roof needed repairs at that time.

A large terracotta female torso found nearby wears unusual attire, a close fitting, long sleeved bodice below with an overfolded layer of cloth above, lavishly decorated with painted squares and swastikas; she holds the overfold tightly in her right hand. That this imposing figure belonged to the superstructure of a mighty building is shown by the surviving join to the roofing system (rooftile) at her back; the torso is stylistically at home in the third quarter of the sixth century, and it is therefore tempting to associate her with the basilica. Similar and contemporary use of decorative figures to highlight the corners of important buildings may be found in Asia Minor, for example, at Miletus; and the connection between Miletus and Sybaris (and hence Poseidonia) is well known.

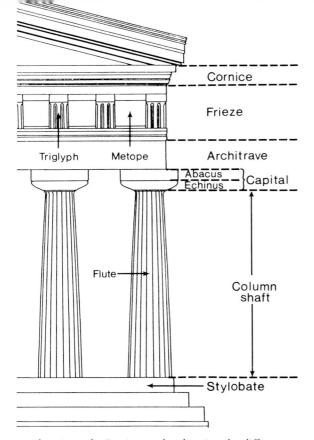

19 Elevation of a Doric temple, showing the different architectural members. (This drawing represents the elevation of the temple in the Heraion at Foce del Sele.)

20, 21 (top) Detail of the top of fluted column shaft and capital showing decorative register of palmettes, rosettes, and tendrils on the echinus. (above) Detail of interior of west façade, showing capitals, architrave course with cuttings for roof beams, sandstone string course and frieze backers.

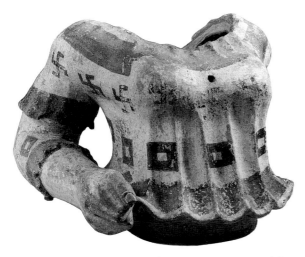

22 Architectural terracotta (there is a join to a rooftile at the back) in the form of a female torso, third quarter of the sixth century BC. The figure wears an unusual garment – a longsleeved bodice beneath a decorated upper blouse – and may have adorned a corner of the superstructure of the temple.

Opposite
23–26 (above) Interior, from the west, showing flank colonnades, ambulatory, upstanding surviving columns of the central row in the cella, with porch beyond. (below left) Three columns between antae of the porch; view from the northeast. (centre right) Inscribed silver disk found in the sanctuary of Hera, sixth century BC. Most commentators take the dedication to read 'I am sacred to Hera; strengthen our bows' and to emphasize the warlike character of one of Hera's aspects. (below right) Detail of anta capital of the porch, showing the cylindrical projection along the under edge. This feature finds sure parallels only at Sybaris and Argos and is often cited as a hallmark of northern Peloponnesian architecture.

Temple of Hera I

Another example of sixth-century terracotta sculpture is provided by the shattered fragments (now heavily restored) of a large seated and bearded figure of Zeus (or Poseidon). Richly dressed, this smiling figure comes from the southern sanctuary. He dates to the last quarter of the century; whether he has anything to do with the basilica remains most doubtful.

In the interior, the ambulatory, i.e. the space between the columns and the walls, is exceptionally broad, and the floor here was of tamped earth. In the porch, three columns stood between the *antae*, the end piers of the side walls: the columns between the piers were treated with *entasis* like their counterparts on the exterior of the building. The capitals of the *antae* are particularly noticeable for the roll-like projections along the underside of the edges; these features find sure parallels only in the architecture of the Heraion at Foce del Sele, at Sybaris, and at Argos, and are therefore distinguishably Achaean/Peloponnesian trademarks. The floor of the *cella* was higher than that of the porch as is obvious from the limestone flags of the floor, and from the absence of fluting on column shafts below floor level; it seems that the planners enjoyed a rethink between the time at which the columns were put in place, and the time when the flagstones were laid. Three of the seven columns of the interior still stand, while the capitals of others, lying on the ground, impart a wondrous sense of the bulk of the building and of the masons' skills.

Recent scholarship has attempted to reconcile the unusual plan of the building (uneven number of columns on the front, central dividing colonnade in the *cella*, back space changed from porch to *adyton*) with the evidence of the more conventional superstructure (the architectural terracottas date to *c.* 540 BC) by suggesting two phases of construction. The first, responsible for the plan, would date then to *c.* 570–560 BC, while a second followed some twenty years later. However that may be, the planners' interest everywhere is in variety of plan and elevation, and in rich new decorative effects. In this respect, the builders were a far cry from their contemporaries in mainland Greece and demonstrated a real willingness to experiment. While mainland temple builders were striving for conformity of proportions and structure, their counterparts in Magna Graecia were involved in new variations of structure and decoration, and new arrangements of the plan. The basilica at Poseidonia provides a good example of these architectural impulses.

Other Structures Nearby

In front of the temple stood the large rectangular altar on which, as usual in the Greek world, sacrifices were made. Built of ashlar limestone blocks, its length matched the breadth of the temple and access to the top for priests and acolytes was provided by a lateral staircase. Immediately to the south was the *bothros*, the rectangular pit into which the residues of sacrifices were thrown (the meat was of course eaten). Another Archaic altar, located to the north and differently aligned, was in use at the same time as the basilica, and may argue the existence of an earlier religious building in the space to the north of the temple. Early Archaic architectural terracottas of the first quarter of the sixth century, found near the basilica but not belonging to it, may have come from such a building.

Other dependencies of the great basilica in the sixth century included a small temple to the southwest, or more likely a Treasury, small in scale but with a columned porch, and to the north another temple of elongated plan subsequently built over in the Roman phase by the so-called *curia* building. This temple of which the bedding trenches and a number of blocks still *in situ* have been found effectively describes the Roman violation of religious space at the time of the expansion of the Forum, and probably also provides evidence of the northward extent of the sanctuary in the sixth century. To the west, the approximate line of the boundary of the precinct is provided by the main road, since the visible *temenos* (precinct) wall itself is thought to be later; to the south, the wall of the *temenos* ran parallel to the city wall, as far as can be ascertained, while the boundary to the east is lost beneath the modern highway.

Whose Temple Was It?

What divinity or divinities was housed in the basilica? In Poseidonia, the city of Poseidon whose image appeared dramatically on her early coinage, the god of the sea himself ought to be a prime candidate. But no evidence supports this view. The great preponderance of terracotta votive figurines found in the sanctuary of the sixth century, though retrieved from votive deposits which became mercilessly contaminated by later reorganizations and intrusions, especially in the Roman period, shows female types normally identified as Hera: and the presence of Hera in the sixth century is proved by an inscribed silver disk which declares 'I am sacred to Hera; strengthen our bows'. This introduces an unusual aspect of Hera – Hera the provider and preserver of weapons – and may be placed side by side with the seated terracotta figures holding horses (Hera Hippia) to suggest that the cult was based in the aristocracy; for the raising of horses was a recognized pastime of aristocrats, and only aristocrats could afford four-horse chariots. The votive deposits prove the presence of Hera in later periods too, since, for example, the numerous fragments of black-glaze pottery inscribed with the letters HP and HPA – Greek characters which read HERA – can only have been dedicated to her. So, it seems that Hera was established as the protectress both of the northerly boundary and the city's territory in that direction (at Foce del Sele) and of the city itself at the sanctuary within the walls.

She seems, however, not to have been alone in the sanctuary: an inscribed sandstone *cippus* (a rectangular, flat-topped block) found to the east of the basilica's altar proclaims 'CHIRONOS' = ['I am the *cippus*] of Chiron', and informs us of the existence here in the sixth century of a cult of Chiron, the famous centaur and mentor of no less a hero than Achilles. Moreover, the terracottas which portray the *hierogamia*, the sacred marriage of Zeus and Hera, point to a cult of Zeus; and this is supported by a silver plaque dedicated to Zeus Xenios and found, again, to the east of the altar. Furthermore, the division of the *cella* of the basilica into two equal naves must be significant. The nervousness of early planners about roofing arrangements has been advanced to explain the single row of columns in long narrow *cellas* which are the hallmark of the seventh-century temples at places like Samos and Thermon. No such apprehension is evident at Poseidonia. The *cella* is wide, the two naves are wide, and there is complete mastery of stoneworking; the ambulatory is broad, spans from columns to walls are broad and the conclusion that builders were well versed in bridging ceiling and roof spans is inescapable. The explanation of the twin naves in the *cella* must then be liturgical, and the presence of Hera and Zeus together in this building therefore becomes probable. Alternatively, perhaps we face two aspects of Hera herself: Hera, armed and warlike on the one hand, and Hera the *kourotrophos*, the nurturer, on the other.

The Temple of Athena

The other major sanctuary so far discovered within the city walls, lies in the northern sector of the city, and is famous for another Doric temple of the sixth century. This temple, located at the highest point within the city, faces east and follows the same orientation as its predecessor in the sanctuary of Hera. It is much smaller, measuring *c.* 33 metres in length by *c.* 14.5 metres in breadth, but what it is lacking in size, it makes up for in breathtaking innovations of plan and decoration.

The plan insists on a contrast between the exterior colonnade, which with six columns on the façade and thirteen on the flank anticipates the ideal proportions of the canonical Doric Order of the Classical period, and the unbalanced proportions of the interior mass which provide a very deep porch at the front of the *cella* and no back porch of any description. This emphasis on the importance of the east of the building is underscored by the width of the passage at the front between the exterior columns and the columns of the porch: it is twice the size of the passage at the back. Details of the elevation echo this interest in the approach. The *cella* is a rectangular space with no evidence of interior columns, while the porch boasts eight Ionic columns: two of these are engaged in the *antae* of the porch walls, while four present the façade of the porch, with two on the return. These porch columns are not aligned with those of the external colonnades, a common practice in Magna Graecia, which allowed the interior mass of the temple to float free of the surround, and stress its own identity.

The Doric columns display a distinct *entasis*, though less pronounced than that of the columns of the basilica, and they appear slimmer, more elegant. The lower part of the capitals is decorated with an *anthemion* collar which emulated, perhaps even copied, that on the capitals of the basilica, while the profile of the *echinus*, though certainly convex and somewhat bulbous in the archaic manner, is flatter than that of the capitals of the basilica. Above a conventional architrave, the frieze is framed by unconventional string courses of sandstone lavishly decorated with architectural mouldings which sharply set off the frieze between them. The frieze itself consists of large travertine blocks which present the front planes of undecorated metopes and are cut back to receive sandstone triglyphs, one of which may be seen in the Paestum Museum. Corner metopes were hugely elongated in size and no attention was paid to the perceived need among mainland Greek architects for regularity of dimensions. The problems posed by the contradictory need for triglyphs at the corners and directly over the columns, and for metopes all of equal size were just ignored. Although eighteenth-century drawings show projecting blocks of a horizontal cornice, commentators today propose that, with great bravado, the architects decided to abandon the horizontal cornice of the pediment, thus effectively abolishing any question of sculptural decoration. Rather, they chose to draw attention to the raking cornices which they projected from the front plane of the building and equipped with ornamental soffits. The eaves along the flanks of the building were protected not by terracotta decoration but by sandstone reliefs depicting lionheads (used as spouts) and palmettes.

Columns of the Ionic Order with Ionic volute capitals revolutionized the treatment of the interior; though smaller in scale than the columns of the Doric exterior colonnade, these again signalled the builders' interest in the approach to the holy of holies both by their quantity and their surprising appearance. This is the first building, known to us, in the whole history of architecture, to incorporate both Doric and Ionic together; as such, it is the clear precursor of developments in Attica some fifty years later. Immediately behind the porch provision was made for staircases leading presumably to a landing from which the cult statue could be seen more easily, and routine cleaning both of the building and the statue could be undertaken.

The novelties of the building are numerous: the mix of materials in the frieze and the technological arrangement of triglyphs and metopes; the absence of the horizontal cornice on the ends; the enlarged raking cornices with elaborate soffits; the use of the Ionic Order in the interior. Architectural details, most especially the profile of the capitals, suggest a date of *c.* 500 BC for the construction of the building. It co-ordinates elements of the canonical Doric Order (plan of the colonnade) with specifically West Greek notions (the separation of the colonnade from the central block), and ideas from East Greece (more columns at the east emphasize the approach); but above all, it introduced the Ionic Order, full-blown, into the fabric of the building

Temple of Athena

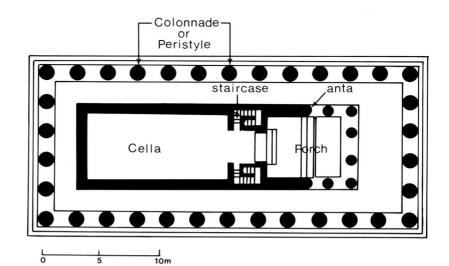

Colonnade
or
Peristyle

staircase   anta

Cella   Porch

0   5   10m

27 (above) *Plan of the temple.*
Noteworthy is the contrast between
the canonical Doric arrangement of
the peristyle (six columns on the
façade by thirteen on the flank) and
the unbalanced arrangement of the
interior space with a large porch at
the east but no trace of a
corresponding back room. Late sixth
century BC.

28 *Detail of interior of west façade,*
showing entasis *of columns, capitals,*
and sandstone string courses framing
the frieze backers.

29 (above) *West façade of temple, entablature showing frieze course (triglyphs to be inserted separately) framed by sandstone string courses, and enlarged raking cornices with elaborate soffits.*

30 *Detail of top of fluted column shaft and capital showing* anthemion *collar decorating the* echinus.

31 *Ionic capital from porch. No less than eight Ionic columns (two engaged, six freestanding) embellished the porch; this is the first building known to us to use both Doric and Ionic columns – an architectural precedent followed at Athens some 50 years later.*

32 Terracotta figurine of Athena, fifth/fourth century BC. *Helmet, aegis, and shield are the identifying attributes.*

(columns and capitals of the porch). Its counterpart in the Greek East is undoubtedly the temple of Athena at Assos: there, the Doric Order was chosen, itself an alien in Asia Minor, but on the normally undecorated architrave on the exterior of the building, below the conventional triglyph and metope frieze, a continuous sculptured frieze in the Ionic manner was added, so that planners here too were already toying with the balance between Doric structure and Ionic decorative elements. These two temples, then – at opposite ends of the Greek world – stood as exemplars of radical temple planning which led ultimately, in terms of a felt need to balance Doric and Ionic elements, to the Hephaisteion and the Parthenon at Athens.

Though still known colloquially as the Temple of Ceres – another misnomer attributable to eighteenth-century dreamers – the temple was dedicated to Athena. A votive deposit south of the temple, miraculously undisturbed, yielded terracotta figurines datable to the late sixth and early fifth century, recognizable as Athena, properly equipped with helmet, shield and aegis. The figurines continued into the Hellenistic period, and if any doubt remained, it was dispelled by the appearance of a fragment of Roman pottery bearing the inscription MENERVA. Figures of a seated female deity with a child (a *Kourotrophos* type) also were dedicated in the sanctuary's earliest phase together with figures of a standing bellicose female (a *Promachos* type); these groups of figurines confirm the identity of the divinity. As in the sanctuary to the south, where different aspects of Hera are recognizable, here too Athena appeared in two guises, as the warlike protector of the city, and as the great nourisher. Later groups of votives, of the Hellenistic period, suggest the worship of Aphrodite and Dionysos in the vicinity: nude female figurines, hermaphrodites, *erotes*.

Other Monuments and the Later Temple

The sanctuary occupies the highest point of the travertine shelf on which the city sits: hardly an acropolis, it was nevertheless appropriate for Athena. Painted architectural terracottas with alphabetic inscriptions (coroplasts' marks) in the Achaean script, datable to the first quarter of the century, probably belonged to a small temple to the south of the Temple of Athena; of this, otherwise, only the foundations are preserved. Another early monument in the sanctuary is the votive Doric column and capital now reconstituted on its original three-step base to the northeast of the (later) temple. The capital and most of the drums of the column had been cannibalized and reused in a medieval wall from which they were extracted. To judge from the degree of *entasis* of the column, and the profile of the echinus of the capital, this column was erected *c.* 550 BC. Another larger column stood on a similar base nearby, though none of its drums has been recognized, while a massive altar stood directly in front of the temple with its adjacent *bothros*, the pit for sacrificial residue, immediately behind.

The later history of the temple is not without interest: in the sixth and seventh centuries AD the temple served as a Christian church, as the inhabitants, reduced in numbers, began to congregate around the highest point of the ancient town. Buildings of the classical city were dismembered to build a new village clustered around the church, and from these medieval structures came many classical blocks including the drums of the votive Doric column and the Ionic capitals from the porch of the Temple itself. In the southern ambulatory, tombs were built against the wall of the *cella*, and it is clear that the old Temple of Athena became a religious centre for a contracting Christian community.

33 Metope from the Heraion at Foce del Sele, showing the suicide of Ajax. Notable Greek protagonist at Troy, Ajax is shown falling on his sword. His loss of the contest with Odysseus for possession of the arms of Achilles probably caused his death.

CHAPTER FOUR

THE SANCTUARY AT THE MOUTH OF THE RIVER SELE

Sources and Location

Strabo, the ancient geographer, and Pliny, that indefatigable observer of his life and times, and Solinus, another geographer, record a tradition which claimed that in the course of their wanderings Jason and the Argonauts landed near the river Sele, and founded there a sanctuary to Argive Hera. This distant echo, relayed to Strabo and others, may reflect a tradition of pre-Greek settlement here: the Sele is the only major river which debouches into the sea in the whole of the coast from Salerno to Agropoli and the mouth of the river would therefore have been an obvious port of call for Bronze Age seafarers. In any event, for local minds, the foundation of the sanctuary took place long ago, and the founders came from abroad. Since the eighteenth century explorers have marched up and down and around the course of the Sele, Strabo in hand, in a fruitless search for the sanctuary; and it was not until 1934 that Paola Zancani-Montuoro and Umberto Zanotti-Bianco made their exciting discovery. Not only did they locate the sanctuary, they unearthed altars and temples and the other paraphernalia of sanctuary life, among which was a whole gallery of sculptured stone metopes which may fairly claim to be the most majestic documents of West Greek sculpture ever retrieved.

Strabo's description claims that the sanctuary is on the left-hand side of the river (which it is) while Pliny says that it is in the Ager Picentinus, hence on the right-hand side (following the direction of the flow) and north of the Sele. How Pliny got it wrong is a matter of speculation: one must assume either that his source was misinformed or that he confused his notes. He does tend to make errors like this. In any event, the sanctuary is to the south of the river, c. 1 mile (1.6 km) nowadays from the mouth, and about 5.5 miles or 8.5 km (Strabo: 50 stades) from the city. It was linked to the north Gate of the city, the Porta Aurea, by a road, evidently intended for pilgrims, and stood as the northmost marker of Poseidonia's territory.

Little is visible today, the site being overgrown for the most part, but rich in snakes; foundations of major structures are however discernible, and the focal points are recognizable: a temple, altars, porticoes, a treasury. Unusual is the building, square in plan, the 'Edificio Quadrato'. The full extent of

61

the sanctuary is not known, but trial trenches opened *c.* 300 metres and *c.* 500 metres to the east have found other buildings and reused metopes. New excavations, begun in 1987, may give us the size of the sanctuary.

Minor Monuments

Two altars stand in front of the temple, some 30 metres to the east, neither being truly aligned with the temple or with one another; alignments, in fact, in this sanctuary seem alarmingly haphazard. The altars are rectangular, large, stonebuilt, and provided with steps in front. To the north, two long skinny colonnaded buildings provided rest and shelter for visitors; these are *stoai*, familiar edifices in sanctuaries throughout the Greek world. One of these, dated *c.* 580 BC by the excavators, is the oldest building in the sanctuary; this was replaced in the fourth century BC by a dogleg-shaped portico adjacent. The 'Edificio Quadrato', similarly built in the fourth century according to the excavators, is square in plan and reused Archaic materials in its construction: its shape argues somewhat against its having a religious function, but it was furnished with a handsome door and vestibule on the south side. Could it have been a dwelling for priests or the offices of the sanctuary?

The Treasury and Its Metopes

Of the Treasury (perhaps itself a small temple), slight remains survive: the foundations of three walls – though no trace of the fourth – are situated a few metres north of the temple. It seems to have been a prostyle building, of which luckily enough examples of the column capitals and of the *anta* capitals have been found. The Doric capital has a flattened *echinus*, while the *anta* capital is lavishly decorated on the face with a register of lotus and palmettes, themselves framed by architectural mouldings; moreover, attached to the underside of the edge is the decorated cylindrical roll of the type which, as we have seen, also adorns the *anta* capitals of the basilica within the city. This is the so-called 'sofa' capital, parallels for which may be found in Sybaris and Argos and perhaps also at Metapontum. This is clear evidence once again, in the architectural detail, of Achaean/Argive derivation. The great glory of the building was, however, the Doric frieze with its triglyphs and sculptured sandstone metopes, of which many have survived. Most were used in the building materials in new structures of the fourth century, and being sandstone avoided the attention of the medieval limeburners whose kiln was found south of the temple; these graceless artisans were doubtless responsible for the wholesale disappearance of most of the stone masonry in the sanctuary.

The excavation in the 1930s pulled out no less than thirty-three stylistically similar metopes, and fragments of another (or others); and though most were

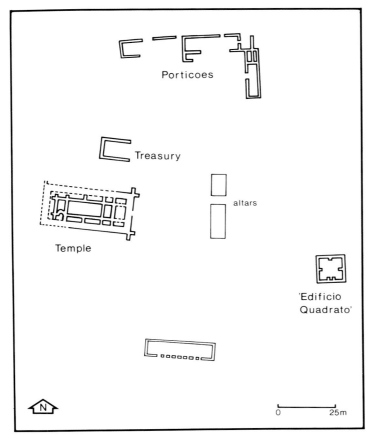

34 Plan of the sanctuary of Hera at Foce del Sele, showing temple, treasury, porticoes, altars and fourth century 'Edifico Quadrato'.

found reused in later buildings, one or two came to light close to the Treasury itself. On this basis, all are associated with the building; moreover, Corinthian pottery from the foundation fills beneath the building suggests a date of *c.* 570–*c.* 560 BC for the construction of the building, and the style of the metopes fits well with this chronology; furthermore, many of the metopes seem to be thematically linked.

The detailed publication of the Treasury appeared in 1954: architectural evidence for only three of the four walls was found giving the width of the building, but not the length. The width allowed the positioning of six of the metopes on the façade, and six on the back, with the assumption of twelve on either flank; this assumption, based obviously on the number of metopes and fragments retrieved, and on probable proportions of length to breadth of such a building in the second quarter of the sixth century, implied that almost the entire frieze had been found. The Museum at Paestum was built

Herakles Metopes

Above, left to right

35 Herakles delivers the Erymanthian boar (one of the twelve labours) alive to Eurystheus who surveys the animal from the safety of a storage jar. The heroic scene is here enlivened by good natured humour.

36 Herakles carries the Kerkopes bound hand and foot on a pole slung over his shoulder. Mischievous gnomes from the island of Ischia (near Naples), the Kerkopes stole from Herakles while he slept. Herakles caught them, as the metope shows, but let them go because they made him laugh with scurrilous remarks about his hairy backside which they were uniquely well situated to observe.

37 Herakles in the act of slaughtering Alkyoneus, son of Ouranos (the Heaven) and Ge (the Earth) and the most potent of the monstrous Giants who had the gall to attack the gods. Note the short torsoes and muscular limbs, perhaps hallmarks of a Peloponnesian workshop.

38 Herakles (with club) and Apollo struggle for the Delphic tripod, seat (literally) of the priestess of Apollo whenever oracular responses were delivered.

39 (left) Metope from the Heraion at Foce del Sele showing Herakles wrestling with the Libyan giant, Antaios. The cutout two-dimensional figures suggest the metope may have been finished with paint, or left unfinished.

in the first place to house this magnificent series of metopes, along with the other materials from the sanctuary at Foce del Sele, and the Entrance Hall to the Museum majestically displays a built facsimile of the exterior of the Treasury with the metopes slotted into the reconstituted frieze. A staircase and gallery on the exterior of the reconstruction allow the visitor to climb to the level of the frieze and see the metopes at close quarters. Many of the metopes were worked from the same sandstone block as their accompanying triglyphs, and the upward tapering of the blocks and cuttings to accommodate roof beams emphasize clearly enough the architectural, as well as emblematic, function of the frieze. The reconstruction in the Museum reflects the conclusions drawn in the 1954 publication, and makes, by its size and sculptural intensity, an overwhelming impression on the visitor.

More excavation in the sanctuary in 1958 produced three other stylistically similar metopes; and the discovery, of course, brings into question the supposed length of the building and the conjectured arrangement of the metopes in the frieze. It may be that the assumed length of the building is accurate; and in this case that the appearance of more metopes means more buildings with sculptured decoration, the location of which is as yet unknown, or that those metopes which present figures only in outline (e.g. the panel showing the Suicide of Ajax) were unfinished and never used. On the other hand, it may be that the building was longer than the excavators thought, and that metopes which seem schematic and unfinished, were in fact finished with paint.

There is no uncertainty about the width of the building or that it would and did accommodate six metopes. The metope depicting the centaur Pholos, more human than other centaurs and shown with human face, body and limbs and bestial only at the back, was found in front of the building where it had fallen from the façade. On this basis, the excavators suggested that five other metopes showing centaurs and Herakles belonged to the east façade and that they represented the battle between Herakles and the centaurs at the cave of Pholos. There can be no doubt about this. In terms of its sculptural programme, then, the façade of the Treasury presented a single, unified theme. Other narrative themes can be detected among the metopes: there is a whole series showing other exploits of Herakles.

Some of these are well-known in the Greek decorative vocabulary (Herakles and his wrestling match with the Libyan giant, Antaios; Herakles bringing the captive boar to king Eurystheus who has leapt in alarm into a capacious storage jar), others less so (Herakles and the trussed up Kerkopes, sprites who had robbed him in his sleep; Herakles killing Alkyoneus, the mightiest of the giants). Other episodes in which the archetypal hero was involved are eminently recognizable: the struggle with the monstrous serpent, the Lernaean hydra; the combat with the Nemean lion; the dragging of the hound Kerberos from the gates of Hades; the fight with Acheloos, the largest river in Greece, over the princess Deianira; the battle with the centaur Nessos who also took

40 Metope from the Heraion at Foce del Sele. Troilos, son of Priam (king of Troy) and Hecuba, seeks sanctuary in a temple, and implores Achilles with the conventional gesture grasping his (Achilles') beard. Achilles, pitiless, delivers the blow.

a liking to Deianira; the struggle with Apollo for the Delphi tripod, and the defence of Hera. The defence of Hera against the Sileni and the combat with Nessos are given particular prominence, each episode being depicted in three narratively connected metopes, while a single metope sufficed for other incidents.

Given the programmatic appearance of the east façade's arrangement of the metopes, and the distinctive prominence of Herakles, it seems highly likely that the other metopes showing Herakles' endeavours formed a cycle, and appeared as such (i.e. next to one another in the frieze). Recent scholarship has proposed that fifteen metopes depicting Herakles' efforts can be identified and may be positioned on the south frieze. Other metopes, similarly, may be interpreted as representing a cycle: the cycle in this instance is epic and concerns the war at Troy and its aftermath. Scenes depicted on one or more panels apparently include Zeus enthroned, Achilles and Troilos, Eris (the goddess of strife), Hektor and Patroklos, the funeral of Hektor, the suicide of Ajax, the murder of Agamemnon, Orestes' revenge. If a Herakles cycle appeared on one long side of the building, it would be fitting that an epic cycle should provide a counterpart on the other.

Some metopes stand on their own, unrelated to others: Sisyphos rolling his boulder uphill with a winged demon on his back; a seated figure (Odysseus?) riding on a turtle. Others appear in pairs: e.g. Apollo and Artemis shooting arrows in one metope at Tityos, who has taken one missile in the forehead already, as he carries off their mother, Leto, in another. The programme of the whole building evidently called for a mixture of metopes depicting cycles (on the east, north and south, perhaps) and metopes depicting single incidents either in single metopes or in twos (at the back).

In terms of the development of the Doric frieze, the Treasury at Foce del Sele represents a pictorial breakthrough. In the Classical period cycles were to become normal on Doric friezes (e.g. the Parthenon) and they were already popular by the end of the sixth century (the Treasury of the Athenians at Delphi). The Treasury of the Sikyonians at Delphi, dated contemporaneously with the Treasury at Foce del Sele, offers metopes connected across a triglyph, but otherwise isolated incidents appear to be portrayed, and there is no cycle as such. Other early buildings which boasted Doric friezes, such as the Temple of Apollo at Thermon or Temple C at Selinus in Sicily, though less well preserved than the Treasury at Foce del Sele, were apparently decorated with metopes seemingly unrelated in subject matter. It seems that the use of a cycle of events as the emblematic matter in the Doric frieze was an innovation which took place in the Greek West, and, in spite of the accidents of survival, the discoveries at Foce del Sele may allow the conjecture that it was artists working at and near Poseidonia who played a leading role in this development.

The condition of the metopes varies greatly; some are fragmentary and only partly preserved, but most are complete though wholly repaired from broken pieces. Some are in high relief, some in low, while others present figures as contours in almost two dimensional, cut-out style. The appearance of the cut-out, cartoon type has led to the theory that these panels were unfinished, and were left in this condition either because the builders were in a hurry to get them in position or because the artists moved away. It is easier to imagine, in this age of experimentation, artists enthused with the idea of filling in the details, and introducing three-dimensionality, in paint. Whatever the reasons for the rather two-dimensional metopes, they serve to emphasize the pictorial origins of the decorated metope (painted terracotta in trabeated architecture); and the series as a whole documents the varying artistic approaches of which, of course, the high relief is ultimately the most popular. The relief is so high by the mid-fifth century, in fact, that some figures appear entirely in the round, as in the metopes of the Parthenon; and if this is seen as the victory of mass over design, paint continued to be used lavishly even when high relief was the order of the day.

The iconographic repertoire of the metopes was for the most part common to the Greek world of the sixth century. The exploits of Herakles, the Trojan War, the dread fates of Agamemnon, Aegisthos and the house of Atreus

41 Metope from the Heraion at Foce del Sele. Greedy and devious in life, Sisyphos, according to Homer, was obliged in death to roll a boulder up a hill, only for it to roll down again. This metope shows the endless punishment, Sisyphos, hag-ridden by a winged demon.

were myths firmly etched in the Greek mind. Yet some episodes seem more at home in the Greek West than elsewhere. Herakles and the Kerkopes, thievish, tricky gnomes who lived on the island of Ischia, enjoyed a particular vogue in Sicily and South Italy, while the figure riding the turtle continues to baffle and amuse. Without contemporary parallel so far, the scene appears later, but rarely, in vase-painting and on Etruscan mirrors. Can this turtle-riding figure be Odysseus? For the metope makers at Foce del Sele, the literary and oral record is the obvious source for some of these myths; and for the less common and those more admired in the West, the lost epic, *Kerberos*, by Stesichoros of Himera, who flourished *c.* 600 BC, is often invoked. Figurative prototypes must also have played a part. The chest of Kypselos, tyrant of Corinth in the middle of the seventh century BC, at Olympia described in such detail by Pausanias in the second century AD would have offered one visual source. Decorated with registers of scenes carved in the cedarwood and picked out with appliqués of gold and ivory, Kypselos' gift offered a veritable encyclopaedia of figural themes: adventures of Homeric heroes, contests and games (suitable at Olympia), themes of violence and deceit. The walls of the Temple of Athena Chalkioikos at Sparta adorned with bronze panels describing the adventures of Herakles and the Dioskouroi – Castor and Pollux – who received divine honours at

Sparta and participated among other exploits in the voyage of the Argonauts, would have provided another. Greek sculptors travelled widely in the sixth century, as the signature of Bion of Miletus at Delphi testifies, so there is every reason to think that sculptors from West Greece too would have visited mainland sanctuaries. Alternatively, and closer to home, the sculptors at Foce del Sele could have drawn on relief scenes such as those displayed in registers (Gorgons on the Run; Homeric combats; Menelaos and Helen?) on the seventh-century terracotta *perirrhanterion* (purification basin) from Incoronata, near Metapontum. And figural scenes doubtless appeared on paintings and textiles now lost. Or should we think of pattern books circulating?

In this context it is convenient to recall the settlers' origins, and any myths of particular potency in the Argolid and at Troizen. Pliny identifies the divinity worshipped at Foce del Sele as the Hera of Argos; so, the presence of Zeus and Hera and the exploits of Herakles (=Hera's glory, the hero whose successes honoured Hera) in the metopes has a possible connection with the distant Argolid. Moreover, some of Herakles' adventures took place in the Argolid (e.g. the Nemean lion) and the centrality of the Argolid in the Trojan War and subsequent events (at Mycenae) is obvious. As to Troizen itself, located in the eastern Argolid, the traditional record claims that this is the place at which Herakles appeared from Hades with the wretched Kerberos (Stesichoros of Himera's *Kerberos* comes to mind again); while another local story has it that Orestes was purified there. Kerberos and Orestes are important images in the metopes, and the historical connection of Poseidonia and Foce del Sele with Troizen offers a possible explanation of the appearance of these myths.

The style and subject matter of the figures reflect a melange of impulses at work. Even where the relief is highest the technique is brusque and without modelling, relying on the progressive cutting back of horizontal planes, drawing out the contours, and depending on paint for details. Robust bodies with short torsos and muscled limbs, and shapes of heads and eyes recall sculptures from the northern Peloponnese, not least the famous twins Cleobis and Biton dedicated at Delphi by the Argives. On the other hand, some details of drapery are reminiscent of sculptural tricks recently associated with the famous studio on the island of Chios, and hence with East Greek influence; while in terms of themes the Silenus type is unknown in the Peloponnese, and may point to local West Greek interest or traditions. In this blend of models, or sources of inspiration, from various areas of the Greek world, and in their enthusiastic experimentation with technique, the metopes at Foce del Sele stand as a sculptural counterpart to the architecture of the basilica at Poseidonia. We glimpse an exhilarating picture of innovations in architecture and sculpture being implemented perhaps within a single generation; granted a chronological gap of say twenty years between the building of the Treasury at Foce del Sele and the basilica at Poseidonia, could the same workshop of artisans have been responsible for both? How are we to interpret the absence of metopes from the basilica (and indeed elsewhere in the city itself) and their commanding presence in Hera's sanctuary 5.5 miles (8.5 km) away? It is too far-fetched to see this as a complementary device to signal the cultic identity of the two sanctuaries? What is absent at Poseidonia is present at the Sele; what is absent at the Sele (striking architecture) is present at Poseidonia.

The Temple and Its Metopes

The buildings did not enjoy the stable foundation furnished by the travertine crust for the buildings of Poseidonia herself; they were instead bedded optimistically and solely on the soil. In the case of the Temple, however, an added precaution was taken; a layer of sea sand was put down over the soil. The temple, of the Doric Order, showed eight columns on the façade and seventeen on the flank; the ambulatory is broad; the porch had two Ionic columns between the *antae*, the ends of the lateral walls, themselves decorated with half columns; the rectangular *cella* measures *c.* 15 × 6 m, and an *adyton* (closed space) at the back balances the porch in front. A number of column drums, some of sandstone and some of limestone were found together with examples of the Doric capitals; the profile of the *echinus* is convex, but flattened, and chimes well with a date of *c.* 500 BC for the building. The frieze course featured sculptured stone metopes the principal motif of which seems to have been pairs of dancing maidens moving to the (viewer's) right. Above the frieze course ran sandstone eaves with lionhead spouts in the conventional manner.

The metopes are quite unlike those of the Treasury. The material, sandstone, is the same; but style and subject matter are wholly different. Pairs of maidens advance in unison to the right with animated gait and gesture; left arms thrown forward they bowl along together, almost dancing. A single female leads them, head turned to face her followers. Though the anatomy of further figures (of a pair) is occasionally bizarre and unconvincing, the style is distinguished for its rich modelling, complexity of surfaces, and intricate presentation of receding planes; shared with the metopes from the Treasury is the worldwide archaic convention of presenting profile heads and legs with frontal torsos. Paint was added in the conventional manner, but this is true three-dimensional sculpture evoking effects of light and shade. The maidens, wearing garments typical of the Greek East, remind us that Velia was founded nearby to the south by fugitives from Phocaia in Asia Minor *c.* 540 BC, while the Temple was built *c.* 500. The figure of the 'leader of the chorus' points even more tellingly to East Greek sources; the high-pointed skull is recognized as a hallmark of northeast Greek sculpture (the area of Phocaia), while muscular arms and emphatic breasts recall the early traditions, again, of Chios.

71

42 Terracotta group of dancing women from the sanctuary at Foce del Sele, probably c. 600 BC. Flattened figures, arranged in a circle were enlivened by added paint.

The appearance of relief sculptures decorating the exterior of these sixth-century buildings is in sharp contrast, as already noted, to the treatment of the sixth-century temples at Poseidonia proper. There, whether in terms of the basilica or in terms of the Temple of Athena, the decoration was confined to combinations of materials (sandstone and travertine) and the glorious proliferation of architectural mouldings together with variations in the elevations. No sculpted metopes have been found. Here, whether in terms of the Treasury or of the Temple, it is the sculptured metopes which take pride of place. The intention can only have been deliberate: on the one hand, to emphasize the city's architectural prowess by bold, complex and imaginative innovations in both plan and elevation of the temples; and, on

43 Terracotta lamp supported by standing women, from the sanctuary of Hera at Foce del Sele. Daedalic hairstyles suggest a date towards the end of the seventh century; gestures with hands framing breasts, point to oriental prototypes or at any rate eastern influences at work (Astarte).

the other hand, to emphasize the importance of the most imposing sanctuary outside the city walls by the programmes of sculpted stone metopes, religious and artistic blazons of enormous consequence.

Votives

Pottery of the late seventh century imported from Corinth, and terracotta figurines of the same date are the oldest materials from the site and confirm that the foundation of this sanctuary and of the city are as good as contemporaneous. Among the oldest terracotta gifts to the sanctuary, two are pre-eminent. First, four plank-like female figures form a circle facing inward and perform a ritual dance; rapidly worked and somewhat formless, this group was enlivened by bright paint of which traces remain. The second is another group of ladies, again forming a circle, though this time facing outward, to engage the viewer; they support and are the ornamental attachments to a lamp; their Daedalic hairstyles date them not much later than c. 600 BC while their gestures (hands raised to frame the breasts) point to oriental influences at work. The votive terracotta figurines confirm that the divinity worshipped here was Hera. The types are well-known: enthroned and holding a child, or sometimes a pony (archaic), enthroned and holding a pomegranate and/or *patera* (a bowl) or basket (classical), nude and kneeling *genii* at her shoulders (fourth century). Most of these figurines were found in votive pits (*stipi*); it was evidently the practice to gather together votive offerings from time to time and bury them in hallowed ground. This both preserved the sanctity of the ancient objects and freed the sanctuary of clutter. Such consecrated ground is called a *stipe* and was sometimes built of rectangular stone slabs; *stipi* in this sanctuary have yielded more than twenty-five thousand terracotta figurines.

Of the figurines representing Hera, and dedicated to her by pious devotees, the most enduring images are those of a seated divinity with a child in her arms, and another, similarly seated, with pomegranate in hand. These pagan icons, live testimony to Hera's interest in fertility (the pomegranate) and powers of human reproduction, survived the centuries to be adopted by the Christian church. Conversion was the object. A church of the eighth century, followed by another close by of the twelfth, was built on the slopes of the hills behind Paestum leading to Capaccio Vecchio. These buildings honoured the Virgin, here persuasively named the Madonna of the Pomegranate; she appears seated with a child held in one arm and with a pomegranate in the other hand. Thus Greek iconography was put to work in the service of the church, and testifies to the wide-ranging influence of Hera's image long after her temples went out of use.

Later Events

The period of maximum prosperity of the sanctuary at Foce del Sele was the sixth and fifth centuries BC, when we may imagine crowds of worshippers arriving either by sea or by the ceremonial road from Poseidonia. About 400 BC the sanctuary suffered a devastating blow; the temple and treasury were severely damaged, and there is much evidence of burning. It is difficult not to associate this with the activities of the marauding Italic tribes who came down from the hills at about this time to take control of many Greek and Etruscan cities (Capua was one, Etruscan; Poseidonia another). Religious life however continued, as buildings newly constructed during the fourth century show; these buildings made constructive use of blocks, including metope blocks, from the destroyed or damaged archaic structures. The arrival of the Romans in Poseidonia (now to become Paestum) in 273 BC signalled renewed damage to the sanctuary which then seemed to enter on a period of long, slow decline. Damaged by earthquake around the middle of the first century AD, the complex fell victim to the volcanic eruption of Vesuvius in AD 79. The presence of volcanic ash is described by the excavators as *visibilissimo*, the stratum of volcanic debris measuring *c*. 30 centimetres in depth. Showered with Vesuvian rubbish, the sanctuary struggled to free itself; a hint of fresh activity is registered in the second century AD, but thereafter swamps and undergrowth began to encroach. The great sanctuary of Argive Hera at the mouth of the rive Sele sank into the oblivion from which it was rescued only by the extraordinary talents of Paola Zancani-Montuoro and Umberto Zanotti-Bianco some 50 years ago.

44 This metope from the frieze course of the Temple illustrates the sharp contrast with those of the Treasury. Here are no great events from myth and legend, but rather a gentle procession of maidens moving in pairs, their arms extended, the clear impression of movement suggested by the position of legs and feet.

45 Fortification system. Section of east wall with east gate (Porta Sirena) from east.

CHAPTER FIVE

POSEIDONIA IN THE FIFTH CENTURY

Walls and Gates

Poseidonia had prospered in the sixth century. The audacious siting of the city betokens settlers of conviction and purpose, and the temples and other public buildings which rose on the city's rocky platform are witness to her citizens' success. A massive defensive system grew up around the town, perched on the edge of the calcareous platform: since the location of the new city was not protected by nature (an island, a peninsula, an acropolis) man-made devices were called for. The walls describe an irregular polygon, their line dictated by the configuration of the travertine crust which rises above the level of the plain at this point. They are difficult to date with any precision beyond the fact that one stretch seems to be Greek since blocks are sometimes, according to Sestieri, inscribed with Greek lettering of the Archaic period (a length to the west of the Porta Aurea, the north gate). The foundations of another stretch, later replaced, appear at the South and also may go back to the Greek period. It is evident, too, that much of the technique of construction is Greek; and equally obvious that the perimeter was built in stages and that there were many repairs and improvements. Some commentators ascribe the layout and original phase of construction to the fifth century; others refer the greater part of the building to the fourth. We must, however, in this context await the report of a team of German scholars; it may be that much more is Roman, following Greek techniques, than is currently thought (see Chapter 7).

The walls are built of ashlar limestone blocks, dry laid; courses of masonry vary in height with irregular alternations of headers and stretchers. They consist of two curtain walls, an inner and an outer, linked at regular intervals by transverse walls with the spaces between the curtains filled with earth. This is a typically Greek way of building fortifications. Thickness of the walls varies between 5 and 7 m; they run for almost 3 miles (4.8 km), a handsome walk, and are punctuated at the points of the compass by four gates, the Porta Aurea (to the north), the Porta Sirena (to the east), the Porta Giustizia (to the south) and the Porta Marina (to the west). Small passages, aligned with the street-grid of the city, also run through the width of the walls. These sally-ports, as they are sometimes called, aimed for ease of exit in quiet times and difficulty of entrance in time of war; some are of the post and lintel variety, others are vaulted. The wall is strengthened every so often by towers, circular, semicircular, or rectangular – there is even a five-sider in the south wall – the most conspicuous examples of which flank the Porta Marina. These towers were either butted up against the walls, or incorporated in their width. Most of them were heavily reconstructed, in careful manner, in the period from 1929 to 1931.

Both north and south gates were originally flanked by towers, and each gave access to a stonebuilt bridge outside which carried the ancient road across the stream of the Salso. The spring water (the Salso) was here canalized to run along both north and south walls and form a moat; thus, a natural source of water became part of the defensive system. The East Gate, the Porta Sirena, greets the modern-day visitor arriving at the railroad station. The least complex of the gates in plan, it projects massively from the line of the walls, and consists of twin bastions either side a simple arch of fourth-century or Roman date. Staircases inside the bastions lead to a rampart along the top of the walls. The keystone of the arch facing the visitor is decorated in low relief with a figure of a Scylla, mistaken in earlier years iconographically for a Siren; hence the name of the gate.

The west gate, the Porta Marina, provides an exciting example of complex military architecture. It is sited in the wall at an oblique angle in such a way that marksmen on ramparts to the left of the gate could have fired shots at enemies' undefended flanks as they approached – the shield on the left arm, and weapon in the right hand leave the right side vulnerable; this is a time-honoured tradition going back to the Greek Bronze Age as exemplified by the fortress at Mycenae. Massive rectangular towers project from the line of the walls, guard rooms either side flank a large courtyard behind, and a large circular tower is present to the north. The remains of another circular tower to the south suggest that the circular towers represent an early phase of life for the gate, subsequently remodelled and reinforced by the insertion of rectangular towers between the circular. It all has a Hellenistic air about it, but the use of huge ashlar travertine blocks, laid dry, seems to preclude a date later than c. 200 BC. A recent theory suggests that extensive repair took place in the first century BC.

Agora and Bouleuterion

Distinguished archaeological work in recent years by E. Greco and D. Theodorescu has identified the location in the city of the Greek *agora*, meeting place *par excellence* of the fifth-century inhabitants. On the grounds of probable continuity of function, it has been thought that the Greek *agora* lay beneath the Roman Forum; but the discovery of the Greek *bouleuterion* (or *ekklesiasterion*, see below), a place of political assembly, has put paid to this theory, since such a building is invariably in or close to the *agora*.

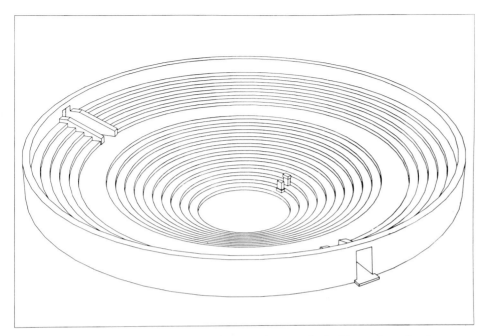

46 Bouleuterion/Ekklesiasterion, restored view. This was the building where the city council or the city assembly (depending on the amount of restoration the reader is willing to countenance) met, and was therefore one of the nerve centres of the Greek polis.

The *agora* is now to be located in the zone immediately to the south of the Temple of Athena; it is bounded to north and south by rises in the profile of the travertine crust, and to the west by a *battuto* (crushed limestone) road found beneath the paved *cardo* of the Roman period. Its eastward extent remains unknown, given the presence of the nefarious S.S.18, the modern highway which bisects the whole of the ancient city. The *bouleuterion* is situated prominently at the eastern edge of the excavated area, while another highly significant building, the so-called Underground Shrine (see Chapter 2) sits close to the western boundary of the newly identified *agora*.

The *bouleuterion* is a round building which provided concentric circles of seats for those attending meetings. These seats were basically steps cut in the travertine shelf, and dressed with cut masonry slabs or blocks. The size of the building, in plan, is impressive but the elevation is difficult to restore, evidence being for the most part missing. One hypothesis, however, proposes that more seats were built above the level of those cut in the rock and that the building would have had a seating capacity of *c*. twelve-hundred. If the building had been so large it may more likely have been the *ekklesiasterion*, the meeting place for the assembly, rather than the *bouleuterion*, the meeting place for the town council. Whether *ekklesiasterion* or *bouleuterion*, it

47 Temples of Hera I and II (beyond), east façades from the southeast. Though larger in dimensions and bulk, and better preserved, the Temple of Hera II displays little of the architectural boldness and creativity typical of its sixth-century counterpart.

presents striking evidence for the political development of the city along democratic lines. Similar structures appear at Acragas and Metapontum.

The building enjoyed a chequered career. It was built around the middle of the century, as material from a pit levelled before construction began indicates. It continued in use after the arrival of the Lucanians c. 400 BC as epigraphic evidence shows: an inscription, found here, uses Greek lettering, but the Oscan language, and records the dedication of a magistrate, Statius, to Jupiter. With the arrival of the Roman colonizers in 273 BC the building was dismantled or destroyed, and the circular hollow in the rock, the core of the building, was filled in with earth, boulders, a huge number of animal bones, and great quantities of sherds and figured terracotta fragments, many of which had not been properly baked and were therefore probably wasters. One view proposes that the huge quantity of ox bones may be interpreted as the residue of an expiatory sacrifice after the building was demolished. Yet the fill deposited in what had been the *bouleuterion* or *ekklesiasterion* of the Greek and Lucanian city bears many of the hallmarks of a rubbish dump: broken pottery, badly fired terracottas, shattered remnants of bellows, industrial refuse all thrown in together. Materials from the fill all date to the end of the fourth century or the first quarter of the third; so the date of the end of the building's life is secure.

Temple of Hera II

The most striking architectural development of the century was the construction of a companion temple to the basilica in the southern sanctuary within the walls: this was the largest of the three great Greek temples. It measured almost 60 × 25 m, preserves all the columns of the peristyle, the superstructure to the level of the horizontal and raking cornices, though the roof is lost, and much of the interior arrangement. There is no need to go to Greece to see Greek temples.

The plan called for six columns on the façade with fourteen on the flank; a porch with two columns *in antis*; the *cella* divided into a nave and two aisles (heralding Christian churches); and a chamber at the back (*opisthodomos*) echoing in plan the porch at the front. The elevation was conventional Doric: three steps to the stylobate, column shafts, capitals, architrave, frieze of triglyphs and metopes, cornices with pediment at front and back. Conventional it was; yet there are absentee elements, the most obvious of which are sculpted stone metopes and pedimental figures. The only hint of a sculpted metope is provided by a marble head of fifth-century date which originally belonged to a relief scene. In the West, marble was scarce, and when stonework was called for, relief groups were often made in limestone with human heads added separately in marble, imported at

48 Temples of Hera I and II (beyond), west façades from the southwest. Separated by one hundred years (construction dates of mid-sixth century for Hera I, mid-fifth for Hera II) the two buildings bear eyewitness to the continuing power of the cult of Hera, and the wealth of the community.

Temple of Hera II

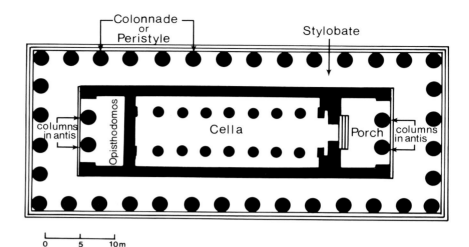

Colonnade or Peristyle

Stylobate

columns in antis

Opisthodomos

Cella

Porch

columns in antis

0 5 10m

49 (above) *Plan of temple. Though there are old-fashioned features (the arrangement of the peristyle with six columns by fourteen, for example), the building is always compared with the Temple of Zeus at Olympia planned by the architect Libon of Elis. Though too (unlike the Olympia temple) it is entirely devoid of sculptural decoration, the use of a number of Doric refinements in the construction suggests the involvement of an architect trained in Greece.*

50 *Porch with two columns in* antis. *This arrangement, typical of classical Doric temples, is repeated in the* opisthodomos *at the back of the building.*

Opposite

51 (above) *West façade from the southwest. Stocky columns show entasis (cigarlike swelling), and were covered with stucco to hide pockmarks in the travertine and to give the appearance of marble.*

52 (below) *Detail of column shaft and capital. The column shaft is equipped with twenty four flutes where twenty might be expected in fully-fledged Doric; this detail and the slightly baggy profile of the* echinus *of the capital hark back to the archaic world.*

53 Marble female head, second quarter of the fifth century BC. Marble was scarce in the Greek west, but the costly material was used for heads inserted into reliefs otherwise made of limestone. Examples exist, for instance at Selinus in Sicily, of sculpted metopes made in this way; this head however is unlikely to be from a metope since (1) only a single other sculpted stone metope has been found in the whole of the city, and (2) it was found in the sanctuary of Athena, far from the Temple of Hera II, the only temple with which it is chronologically compatible.

great expense; such was the case with some of the metopes found at Selinus in Sicily. Yet, this Poseidonian head was found in the northern sanctuary (near the Temple of Athena), and cannot have had anything to do with the great fifth-century temple. In the complete absence of metopes from the sanctuaries, this head is more likely to have come from a relief plaque. The absence of cuttings or remains of clamps in the floor or back of the pediments show that no sculptures were intended here. The temple was to be without decorative sculpture.

VII *Tomb of the Diver, underside of the coffin lid, the diver. Reduced to essentials, the painting focuses on trees, water, the diver and the diving platform. The plunge is from this world to the next, the platform symbolizes the pillar(s) of Herakles, the edge of the known world, and the water the unknown, limitless ocean beyond.*

VIII *Tomb of the Diver, symposiasts. Five figures recline on couches, tables set before them, garlanded and provided with* kylikes *(drinking cups). At right, one young and beardless the other older and bearded, exchange erotic glances. Of the other pair, one turns to watch the courting couple, while his companion crooks the index finger of his right hand around the handle of his* kylix *preparing to hurl the dregs of his wine at an unseen mark (the game was called* kottabos*). The fifth figure admires his drinking cup.*

VII

VIII

The columns of the peristyle are stocky and powerful, and enjoy a slight but perceptible swelling towards the middle (*entasis*); this is far less pronounced, however, than the *entasis* of the columns of the basilica alongside. Each column is carved with twenty-four vertical flutes (twenty becomes the rule in canonical Doric) and all were coated with stucco which both filled in blemishes in the travertine and gave the travertine the appearance of marble. This trick was used on other Greek temples in Poseidonia too and indeed on all Greek temples in the West. Three incised rings decorate the lower part of the *echinus* of each capital. The *echinus* itself retains a slightly baggy profile; it has not yet become the straight-sided abbreviated cone which it became in the High Classical period, whether in Greece itself (as in the Parthenon) or in the West (Temple of Concord at Acragas, for example). The architectural device known as angle contraction is practised at the corners of the building: spacing between columns adjacent to corner columns was narrowed. This became necessary since builders wished (a) to align triglyphs of the frieze with the centres of columns, (b) to push end triglyphs to the corners of the building, and (c) not to have elongated metopes at the corners. The only solution was to contract the whole of the corner of the building.

A short flight of steps preceded the entrance to the *cella* built at a higher level. Either side the entrance doorways gave access to a utility room on one side and to a stairway on the other: from the stairway access was possible to a gallery from which the cult statue could have been observed and maintenance of the ceiling would have been carried out. Within the *cella* two storeys of columns, one atop the other, held the timbers of the ceiling in place, while they also served to divide the space into a nave and two aisles. Cuttings to take the end beams of the rafters of the ceiling may still be seen in the masonry of the *cella* walls. Other cuttings, on the interior of the pediment walls at front and back, were made to take the ends of the beams which were the mainstays of the timber rafter system which held the terracotta tiles of the roof. The two columns *in antis* of the porch are matched at the *opisthodomos* at the west. Floors of travertine slabs are well preserved throughout; since no special provision seems to have been made to articulate the positioning of the cult statue and to take its weight, it is reasonable to assume that the statue was not of stone, and therefore more probably of terracotta.

A number of Doric refinements, or optical corrections, are at play. Since the horizontal line of the stylobate, the course of masonry on which the

---

IX (opposite) *Terracotta figurine of Hera Hippia, sixth century* BC. *Hera appears as the nurturer of horses, symbols of nobility and power throughout the Greek world. This aspect of the goddess may have appealed to the aristocracy since horse-rearing was a favourite occupation of aristocrats, and only they and royalty could afford four-horse chariots.*

columns stand, would appear to sag in the middle if a true horizontal, the stylobate is built to curve *upward* fractionally in the middle; this refinement compensated for any visual distortion. The same applies to the horizontal cornices beneath the pediments. Column shafts incline slightly inwards (as well as having *entasis*). The rarity of these refinements in the Greek West betokens the presence of architects knowledgeable about developments in Greece, and may even suggest that the temple is the brainchild of a Westerner trained in mainland Greece.

The most frequently cited parallel, or source, for the building is the Temple of Zeus at Olympia, finished, the literary sources imply, by 457 BC. The temple at Poseidonia is notably retrospective in several respects: a plan of six columns on the façade by fourteen on the flank (when canonical Doric would have expected thirteen), the rather squat proportions of columns and entablature emphasizing the weight and bulk of the superstructure, twenty-four flutes of the columns rather than twenty, and the slightly convex profile of the *echinus* of the capital. These features are reminiscent of the archaic world. Yet the reduction in architectural decoration, the use of Doric refinements and the analogy with the temple of Zeus at Olympia are persuasive in placing the temple in the period *c.* 470–460 BC. Dubbed the Temple of Neptune (Poseidon) by early explorers who thought it the oldest, and saw it was the largest of the temples, it is in fact probable, judging from votive materials, that it too was dedicated to Hera.

Votives and Other Monuments

The materials from the votive pits (*stipi*) are hardly homogenous and the pits themselves had been seriously disturbed in antiquity; this seems to have happened in the Roman period when the size of the sanctuary was reduced, the ground level became lower than when the temples were built, and there were opportunities for authorized or random tampering with the pits. Contamination or not, there is precious little among any of the votive deposits to suggest the presence of Poseidon and much to suggest devotion to Hera.

Terracotta figurines represent various types: the seated goddess with plank-like lower body, the seated female with *patera* (bowl) and pomegranate which recalls the description of Polyklitos' Hera of Argos by Pausanias, the seated goddess with babe at her breast. Other votives – small terracotta shields, arrowheads, miniature bronze greaves – draw attention to the warlike aspects of the divinity, yet more to the divinity's interest in reproduction, childbirth, fecundity, nourishment. These different types may reflect different aspects of the same godhead, Hera; or they might reflect the presence of other gods – we know, for example that Zeus was here, worshipped together with Hera, and Demeter and *Kore* too; perhaps Athena was also present. Given the vast preponderance of votives which can be identified as Hera types, and the later appearance (third century) of graffiti on potsherds reading HPA, it is evident that Hera was the major divine personality in the sanctuary. It is most probable then that the grandest surviving temple was dedicated to her; other gods were present in the sanctuary, though Poseidon does not seem to have been among them. This is odd; since, if the place of his worship remains unexcavated in some part of the city (towards the sea?), it is puzzling that temples for him have collapsed while those of Hera (and Zeus) and Athena survive upstanding. Altars stood in front of the temple to the east, with accompanying *bothroi* (pits for residue), statue bases nearby, and other paraphernalia of the sanctuary.

Extramural Sanctuaries

The fifth century saw activity in sanctuaries outside the city walls also. Two of these may be mentioned as examples. In the shadow of the city to the south, in the *località* Santa Venera, recent excavations conducted jointly by the Universities of Michigan and Perugia and the Soprintendenza have taken up the work begun by Pellegrino Sestieri in the early 1950s. An *oikos* temple and a large rectangular hall, perhaps used for ritual dining, have been identified as belonging to the fifth-century sanctuary. Architectural materials were less ambitious than those used *intra muros* with only the lower courses of masonry and the upper of mudbrick, but the plan of the *oikos* was innovative, daring and probably symbolic. A circle of blocks created an unusual space within the *cella*, for which the only analogy seems to be a fifth-century building at Olympia. The divinity here was Aphrodite. Some 10 miles (16 km) to the northeast of Poseidonia, and close to Albanella, recent exploration has unearthed a rural sanctuary typical of the *chora* (territory) of Poseidonia. The architecture is simple, the materials primitive. The sanctuary consists of a rectangular enclosure built of dry-laid fieldstones, small in size, but with large unworked rocks marking the corners of the structure. Entrance is from the west, and the principal features inside are four circular stone-built hearths with much evidence of burning and animal sacrifice. Votive materials allow the tentative identification of the cult here as that of Demeter Thesmophoros.

The Tomb of the Diver

If the temple architecture of Poseidonia assures the city a leading role in the growth and maturation of the Doric Order, with its particular Western gifts of vitality and originality, the city is equally central for our knowledge of Greek painting. It was only twenty years ago (1968) that in the systematic exploration of Greek cemeteries (*necropoleis*), Mario Napoli discovered the painted tomb known as the *Tomba del Tuffatore*, the Tomb of the Diver. It was found in the *località* Tempa del Prete nearly 1 mile (*c.* 1.5 km) south

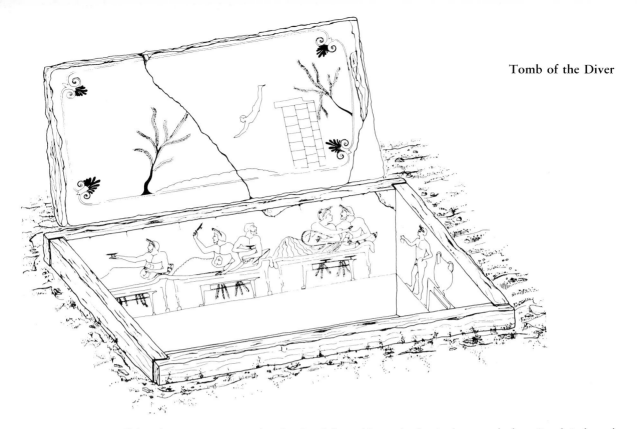

54 Slabs of travertine, stuccoed and painted form this tomb, the single example from South Italy and Sicily of a tomb of the early fifth century BC painted with figured scenes. The date is confirmed by grave goods. The other long side shows another symposium scene, and the other short side three guests, including a flautist. See also colour plates VII, VIII.

55–57 (below) Symposium scene. An entranced couple occupy the central couch flanked by a single figure holding a lyre and an egg, and another couple enjoying a musical moment. (opposite above) Three guests: a bearded male with a stick and an energetic young man follow a girl flautist. Are they coming or going? (opposite below) Single attendant: a nude youth holds an oinochoe *(wine jug) just refilled from the adjacent garlanded* krater *(mixing bowl).*

of the city; it consists of five travertine slabs constituting the four sides and lid of a stone coffin inserted in a rectangular cutting in the rock. Only the floor of the boxlike coffin was unpainted; the deceased, and only he (it was a male burial), was to have the benefit of the bright paintings which decorated walls and ceiling.

Each long side depicts five lounging male figures engaged in banqueting; they recline on three couches positioned behind three low garlanded tables, on one of which stand two drinking cups. On one side, the pair of figures on the couch to the right gaze admiringly at one another, one older and bearded, the other younger and cleanshaven; the older caresses the head of the younger (a musician; he holds a lyre), while the younger strokes the other's chest. Their intentions are obvious. The attention of one of the two reclining on the middle couch is caught by the implied eroticism of this scene; he leans toward the would-be lovers, sitting up on his elbow, black glaze *kylix* in his right hand. His companion faces the other direction, playing *kottabos*; index finger crooked through the handle of his cup, he aims the dregs of his wine at a mark before him. The fifth figure of this side reclines alone, right arm extended in front of him, cup in hand.

On the other long side, another entranced (bearded man and youth) couple occupy the middle couch, flanked to the left by a single figure who watches them with rapt attention, holding a lyre in one hand and an egg in the other. The egg, symbol of fertility and of resurrection, often appears in Greek, Etruscan and Lucanian funerary contexts; it was a favoured emblem among the followers of Pythagoras, whose influence in South Italy grew rapidly after he settled in Croton in the later years of the sixth century. The pair on the couch to the right face the central duo; one of them plays the double flute while the other stares upward, right hand on his head, as if carried away by the melody. If music be the food of love on this long side, it is drinking on the other. Of the two short sides, one shows a nude youth walking to the left and holding an *oinochoe* (wine jug) which he has just replenished from the large garland-bedecked *krater* (mixing bowl) placed on the table behind. The other short side depicts three figures moving to the right: a girl flautist, dressed in white, leads the way, followed by a striding (dancing?) young man and a bearded male figure wearing a mantle and holding a stick. Are they arriving or leaving?

The scene on the underside of the lid of the coffin has given the tomb its name. A naked youth plunges in midair from a diving board at the right into a pool beneath. Head held high, his entry into the water will not be easy. This focal motif is framed by schematic trees, the corners of the slab are marked by four palmettes, and the whole scene is bounded by a thin green border, as if in a picture frame.

The travertine slabs were coated with stucco to give a plain white background for the painted episodes. A broad brown band provides a ground line for the side panels; with the exception of a bright blue used for the textile couch covers and for the mantle of the figure on one short side, all shades are earth colours standing boldly out against the stucco white. Composition is staccato, figures and groups (pairs of banqueters) appear independently and stand free of one another. This figural isolation is epitomized in the panel of the Diver, where all the elements – trees, water, diving platform, diver – command uncluttered space; moreover, description is reduced to essentials, with a bare scaffolding representing the pier or springboard, and trees reduced to minimal stylized trunks and branches. In the painting of the figures, it is the outline which was stressed; within the contours, broad flat washes of single colour predominate with details of musculature, beard or face given graphic emphasis, sometimes even with the use of the burin.

Iconographically, at least two sources seem to be at work. The scenes of banqueting appear on Attic vases of the end of the sixth century and beginning of the fifth (e.g. in the work of the Brygos Painter) while some profiles echo those of the Berlin Painter and his red-figure contemporaries. On the other hand, similar scenes appear in Etruscan tomb-painting. The Diver also has an Etruscan origin. Local inspiration cannot be overlooked: the rural setting for the diver is without parallel, while the striding or dancing figure on one short panel is surprisingly close in posture and gesture to the image of Poseidon on the fifth-century coinage of the city.

A date in the early part of the fifth century (c. 480) is confirmed by the evidence of the grave goods. Few in number, as was usual in the fifth century, an Athenian *lekythos* datable to c. 480 BC and a tortoise shell (perhaps part of a lyre) command attention. Various interpretations may be advanced: the banqueting scenes, with interest in music, dance, wine and sex, reflect patterns of contemporary aristocratic life, and seem to be images of status. On the other hand, they may also be funeral banquets, wakes. The scene on the lid of the tomb may point to the deceased's athletic pursuits, again as emblematic of aristocracy. But, as Bianchi Bandinelli has shown, the symbol is more substantive than that: the plunge is the plunge from life to death, from the edge of the known world, the pillar of Herakles (one only in the fifth century) into the unknown, the ocean.

Much has been made of the connection between these painted tomb panels and Greek wall-painting in the early fifth century. This is natural enough given the plethora of information from literary sources about developments in wall-painting in this period, the high regard in which Greeks of the later fifth century held fresco panel painting and the sparsity of actual recovered examples. Aside from the evidence of the *Tomba del Tuffatore*, the enthusiast has to go to Asia Minor to find any really comparable material (the tomb at Elmali near Xanthos or the painted fragments from Gordion). Yet, caution must be advised. The use of a motif specifically from the Etruscan world (the Diver) suggests local artisans prepared to use foreign motifs and the paintings may not then be totally Greek; and the dependence on other motifs

drawn from the vocabulary of vase-painting implies as much familiarity with, and dependence on, that level of painting as on wall-painting. The style seems fully Greek and archaic, within the boundaries of the vasepainters' skills, so that these panels may be more accurately described as enlargements of painted panels on pots than as reductions of scenes from wallpainting. However that may be – and, given the minimal amount of evidence available, any conclusion must be speculative – this painted tomb justifiably takes its place, alongside the great temples, as another compelling document to the high competence of artists and architects in Poseidonia. There is nothing like it anywhere else in Magna Graecia.

Cemeteries

Other fifth-century burials took place in cemeteries on the periphery of the city: to the north in the *località* Andriuolo, Arcioni and Laghetto, and to the south in the *località* Santa Venera. The *Tomba del Tuffatore* lies south of the large cemetery at Santa Venera which has been the subject of recent, prolonged and informative exploration conducted by the Soprintendenza. There is little variety in the type of grave employed: a rectangle cut precisely in the rock was covered by a flat slab. Occasionally, the sixth-century practice is followed of a grave cut irregularly in the rock and covered with tiles, but this is rare. Sometimes the rectangle cut in the rock receives cut travertine slabs on its four sides, and sometimes these slabs are stuccoed; very rarely the lower part of the stuccoed surface is painted with a red band, as was the case in the *Tuffatore* tomb where the broad red band of paint served as a groundline. Graves are dug at Santa Venera in clearly defined rows along an east-west axis: the overwhelming impression, after the excavation of many graves, is of standardization and a desire for uniformity. In the total absence of literary information about the fifth-century city, the graves and their contents are of paramount importance in deciphering the social and political situation in the city in these years.

Grave goods are few, and in some instances the deceased takes nothing at all with him; there are never more than seven or eight accompanying objects. Nor is there any sign of grave markers, though some means of distinguishing grave from grave seems to our minds essential. Infants and children were buried in the same way as adults, heads to the east, the only

58 (opposite) Athenian black-figure lekythoi, late sixth/early fifth century BC. Lekythoi (oil flasks) were the favoured gift to accompany the dead both in the sixth and fifth centuries; though grave goods in the fifth century were uniformly modest, the popularity of the lekythos *in this context continued unabated.*

59 Athenian red-figure pelike (storage jar), first quarter fifth century BC. The two-handled, large-mouthed, roundbellied pelike *was another popular imported shape among grave goods of the fifth century.*

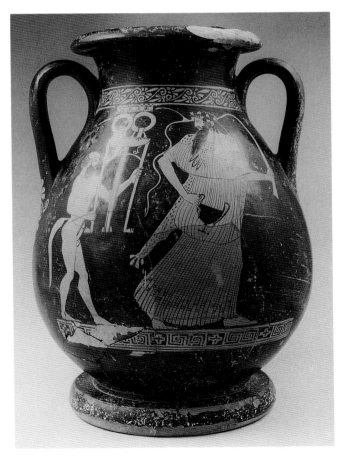

distinction being that the size of the graves was smaller. Male burials are often characterized by the presence of a strigil (a bronze implement for wiping oil off skin) held in the right hand, and an alabaster *alabastron*, an oil flask: these are objects from the world of athletics. No weapons are to be seen. Nor are female burials typified by objects *de luxe*, jewellery or bronze items of adornment. Among vases, the *lekythos* (perfumed oil flask) is the most popular companion along with the *skyphos*, a drinking cup; most of the vases are imports from Athens, either decorated in the red-figure style of the fifth century or in plain black glaze, while some come from other Greek cities in South Italy and others are locally produced copies of imports. The *krater*, a mixing bowl for wine, is not to be found among the grave goods; this conspicuous absence may be significant, since the shape is symptomatic of revelry, banquets and the male world. Sherds of *kraters*, however, and *amphorae* and cups came to light in the excavations of the earth above the tombs: this looks like evidence for ritual libation at the time of burial, or for repeated homages to the dead, or, just conceivably, for grave markers.

What picture of society emerges from these *necropoleis*? Many more tombs remain unopened, so that, in the absence of *all* the evidence, caution is required; yet enough examples have been excavated to allow some comments. Status symbols, whether jewellery for women or weapons for men, are absent from these tombs; together with the uniformity of size and type of grave, this absence seems to suggest levelling social attitudes. The absence of other symbols of the autocracy of the male world (e.g. *kraters*) also suggests the emergence of a distinctly democratic view of society.

The emphasis in male burials on associations with the athletic world is more difficult to read. It might be conjectured that athletics have become a substitute for war, and thus strigils and alabastra have replaced weapons as emblems of status: this seems unconvincing. Or, athletics might be thought of as representing personal effort and suggesting the value of the individual, not the group: athletic connotations might then have a political coloration. Or, since success in athletics depended, as Pindar claimed, on the god-given self-surpassing moment, is the presence of strigils etc. in the graves a nod to the gods?

We are baffled by the absence of any written records. But it is beyond doubt that profound messages are to be sought in this material. It could be that the graves of the wealthy have escaped discovery, and that the simplicity and similarity of these graves and their goods is due, tritely enough, to poverty. On the other hand it could be that metaphysical thought is at work: the control of quality and quantity of grave goods (and total absence sometimes) perhaps reflects society's approach to the next world. On a political level, society is egalitarian and eager to appear so (at any rate, in death) and these developments in ritual practice may be associated with the emergence of a democracy in Poseidonia.

CHAPTER SIX

THE LUCANIAN CONQUEST AND ITS AFTERMATH

The Arrival

As the fifth century closed, Greeks in Poseidonia were keeping a wary eye on their neighbours in the interior. These indigenous peoples, the Samnites, were expanding rapidly in numbers; they were on the lookout for new homes and the Greek and Etruscan cities of the coastal plains were obvious targets. Towards the end of the century, they could restrain themselves no longer; they captured Cumae and Capua in rapid succession, and, at a date which remains uncertain but which must be around 400 BC, they entered Poseidonia and its territory. The local name of these Samnite people was Lucanian, and the city thus ceased to be Greek and became Lucanian. In some ways this change resembles more a fusion of peoples and ideas than a conquest. Greek ways remained, the city continued to be called Poseidonia, since so she is called in the city's glorious fourth-century silver coinage, the *bouleuterion* (or *ekklesiasterion*) remained in use, and the Greek sanctuaries continued to be venerated. Greek continued to be spoken, and in the second half of the century the two outstanding pot painters in the city, Assteas and Python, boasted Greek names, signed themselves in Greek, and did not hesitate to take as themes of their decoration episodes from Greek mythology and from the Greek comic stage.

These archaeological facts rather give the lie to the well-known story told by Aristoxenos of Tarentum, a pupil of Aristotle, to the effect that the Greeks were enslaved, forbidden to speak Greek and only once a year were allowed to congregate at a certain festival where they spoke Greek and complained of their servitude; all this smacks of anti-Lucanian propaganda for a Greek audience. The major changes come in the density of settlement of the territory of Poseidonia and the consequent agriculturalization, in the lavish decoration of tombs and in other burial practices which are sharply different from those of the fifth century and which relish ostentatious display.

The Territory

The territory to which the early Greek settlers staked a claim may be identified from the evidence of sanctuaries and cemeteries. In the sixth and fifth centuries an inner circle of sanctuaries and cemeteries protected,

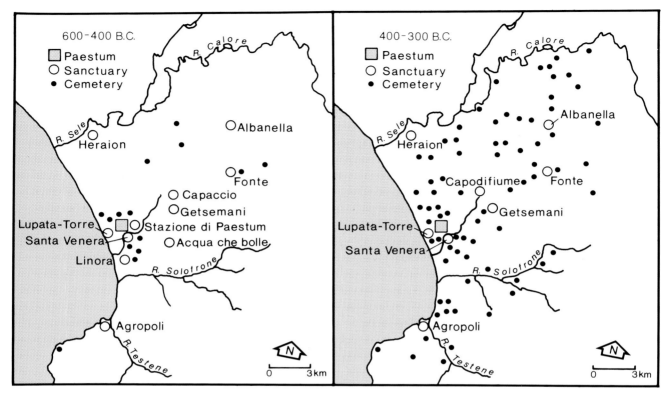

60 Paestum and Territory. Location of sanctuaries and cemeteries between 600 and 400 BC (Greek period, left) and between 400 and 300 BC (Lucanian period, right). In the Greek period sanctuaries mark the boundaries of the territory (Heraion at Foce del Sele, Agropoli) and form protective lines (Capaccio-Getsemani-Acqua che bolle-Linora; and Lupata-Torre-Santa Venera-Stazione di Paestum) in front of the city, while cemeteries in the countryside are few and far between. In the fourth century (right) the plethora of cemeteries in the countryside indicates a density of rural settlement and hence of agriculturalization stimulated by the new occupants of the plain.

naturally enough, the city herself. Sanctuaries at Lupata-Torre, Santa Venera and Stazione di Paestum clustered on the south and east, while the graveyards of Arcioni and Laghetto lay to the north. Another trio, at the very least, of sanctuaries – at Capaccio, Getsemani and Acqua che bolle – were sited to mark control of the plain immediately east of the city up to the foothills. Further to the north and east two other sanctuaries, at Albanella and Fonte, marked the Greeks' claim to access to the passes through the mountains, and to the land within the bend of the river Calore. Major sanctuaries were sited at the northern and southern limits of the territory – the Heraion at Foce del Sele to the north and the sanctuary of Poseidon at Agropoli to the south. Beyond the graveyards close to the city walls, cemeteries in the zones north and east of Poseidonia are few and far between; while none at all have been found to the south in the tract of land between the rivers Solofrone and Testene. The presence or absence of cemeteries is taken to imply the presence or absence of settlements; it seems then that the territory of Poseidonia was only lightly populated.

There was a sharp change in the fourth century. Cemeteries proliferated to the north of the city; they have been found on either bank of the Solofrone directly to the south and either side of the Testene even further south. There are always the accidents of discovery; but the overwhelming number of new fourth-century cemeteries is striking, and the picture is clear. Relatively sparse inhabitation of the territory in the Greek period was followed in the Lucanian by a large increase in the number of people living outside the city. The inference that agriculture flourished and that many people lived and died in the countryside is inescapable.

Sanctuaries and Cemeteries

Architecture does not seem to have commanded a high priority for the newcomers. It is probably toward the end of their period of control of Poseidonia that a rectangular wall was built around the underground shrine built at the end of the sixth century; this new temenos wall served to demarcate the sacred ground and evidently acted both to prevent encroachment and to stress Lucanian enthusiasm for the monument. In the sanctuary of Hera to the south a new small temple with accompanying altar was constructed north of the fifth-century Temple of Hera; little above the foundation levels survives but there is enough to determine the plan. The building had four columns at the front, matched by four at the back, but with none on the flank: tetrastyle amphiprostyle then, and oriented east-west. A deep porch at the east was echoed by a similar porch at the back; behind the porch at the east there is a rectangular room, a vestibule, of about the same dimensions as the porches, and this precedes the *cella* with its flagged floor and base for the cult statue. The plan is eccentric, the cult unknown, the date uncertain.

Votive offerings in sanctuaries continue, for the most part, the terracotta typologies of the Greek period. There are however novelties, some of which represent new or modified Hera types. The new Hera types include an exuberant bust of the goddess, her headgear supporting a huge flower with opening petals which likely acted as an incense burner: Hera as Woman-Flower. Some identify the flower as the lily, itself an icon associated with fecundity because of its amazing reproductive power. Another shows her kneeling and holding a veil over her head, but otherwise nude, with two sprites on her shoulders: Hera Eilytheia, oft invoked for help in childbirth. Other newcomers are piglet carriers, many of whom have been found in the recent excavations at Albanella: the pig is the favoured offering to Demeter in her aspect as *Thesmophoros* (=Bringer of Laws), and pigs were sacrificed in connection with her great festival, the *Thesmophoria*. Female figures carry a piglet in one hand and a cylindrical basket (for cultic objects) on the other shoulder, while males carry a piglet and a platter. The appearance of male

61 *Terracotta female bust (= Hera as flower-woman), fourth century BC. New votive types appear in the fourth century of which many are concerned with childbirth and fecundity, and of which the Hera as flower-woman is one. The headgear and/or veil supports a flower with opening petals which acted as an incense burner. The flower may be the lily, itself extravagantly endowed with reproductive power.*

figures carrying piglets is surprising since the cult of Demeter Thesmophoros was for women only, and prior to the discoveries at Albanella only female piglet carriers had been found in the whole of the Greek West. Thus far, then, this seems like a phenomenon peculiar to Poseidonia. Around 330 BC other new types are introduced from Greece, the so-called Tanagra figurines named thus from their first place of discovery, Tanagra in Boeotia: these were doubtless first introduced into Italy at Tarentum, and distributed therefrom.

The many hundreds of terracotta figurines found at Poseidonia signal a centre of production, surely established as early as the sixth century. For the most part the figurines of the sixth and fifth centuries derive from mould series produced in other Achaean centres (e.g. Metapontum or Sybaris), though they are made, naturally enough, with local clay. Artisans in the city did, however, produce distinctive new types of which the Hera Hippia, a seated female figure holding a horse, is the best known. The fourth century introduced other Paestan types, and new stylistic traits more related to Italic prototypes than to Greek. The Hera as Woman-Flower and the piglet carriers represent new locally produced types; while the seated figure holding a child with her mantle wrapped tight over her shoulders, across her face and round her head offers square features and angular forms more easily paralleled in Italic figures (e.g. from Pontecagnano or Fratte) than Greek.

The most striking signals of the new cultural and political environment are to be found in the cemeteries: in new types of graves, new types of tomb paintings, and new kinds of grave goods. Cemeteries of the fourth century are found on every side of the city, except towards the sea, while the most richly painted have been found, with few exceptions, to the north. No cemetery has been excavated in its entirety so that no conclusions can be drawn about actual size or arrangement of the complexes; most tombs are oriented east-west. Rectangular rock-cut tombs continue, often equipped with four travertine slabs for the sides and a fifth providing a flat lid, though sometimes tiles sufficed for the roof. New, at first, are graves of the same shape but with end blocks extended upward in triangular gable shape; these gables provided the supports for a sloping roof consisting of two slabs leaning against one another, circumflex style. A second new type of grave, introduced after the middle of the century, is the built chamber tomb.

62 Terracotta Tanagra figurine, fourth century BC. *Imported from Greece towards the end of the century, Tanagra figurines were perhaps the most popular and widespread in the Hellenistic world. First found at Tanagra in Boeotia, the figurines take their name from the town.*

Tomb Paintings

The paintings on the walls of the tombs provide the largest, most encompass-ing and the most important gallery of Italic paintings preserved; for variety and range, only those from Capua are comparable. Thanks to the energetic and meticulous excavations of Mario Napoli, the study of the grave goods, and especially the painted pottery, has allowed a progression in painting styles from the early fourth to the early third century to be detected. In a first phase, which dates from *c*. 400–*c*. 370 BC the colour range is still limited, and decorative motifs, for the most part non-figural, are formal and often seem to derive directly from archaic Greek architectural terracottas. The decoration does not distinguish a female burial from a male. Figural representation comes to the fore in the period between *c*. 370 and *c*. 330 BC, and a third phase from *c*. 330 to the first decades of the third century is marked by enlarged figures which make ample use of *chiaroscuro*, a technique known to the Greeks as *skiagraphia*, which doubtless was introduced from Greece or Tarentum at about this time.

The painted panels are blocks of local travertine regularly cut and covered with a thin coating of white stucco which forms the background. Often the dead person, man or woman, is portrayed on the gable part of the end block. If a man, he appears armed and sometimes on horseback which suggests that he may be returning from the battlefield; this is rendered more probable if he is seen to be carrying as well the panoply of a defeated foe ('Return of the Warrior', then); alternatively, he may be seen as embarking on a journey to the next world. Certainly this journey is implied in the representation of a winged cheerful monster-oarsman aboard his vessel who has let down the gangplank ladder and stretches out his arms to a woman coming on board; this figure is evidently the equivalent of the ferryman Charon, and the journey implied is across the Styx; or could we see here an echo of the Etruscan sprite of the dead, Vanth?

Many scenes, whether on the walls of a male or female tomb, refer to funerary rites. Those on long sides sometimes depict funeral games such as chariot races, boxing matches, or armed combat, while others show the deceased on the bier surrounded by mourners. The shorter sides sometimes show mourning women gesturing extravagantly, or funeral processions with sacrificial animals and mourners, or deathbed scenes with mourners, musicians and children. It seems to be the case that when the dead is shown prostrate on the bier or deathbed, it is a woman; but that men appear in

---

X *Lucanian tomb painting: return of the warrior. Plumed helmet, shield, breastplate, belt, greaves (leg guards) were normal equipment for the Lucanian warrior; the black steed, reined in, prances. Is he returning from the battle, or setting out on the journey to the next world?*

X

more heroic circumstances. They are shown mounted on horseback, wearing full armour, taking a cup of wine from a woman, and with a slave behind. The armour worn by these equestrian warriors chimes well with literary descriptions of typical Samnite gear: plumed helmet, cuirass with big shoulder plates, bronze plated belt, greaves. In fact, examples of all these emblems of masculinity and warfare have been found in contemporary tombs.

The origin of these themes is not at all clear; little can be said of the sources of the rite of *prothesis* (laying out the dead) or of funeral games in this Lucanian context, though both chariot races and boxing matches were at home in the Greek world. Figures of Victory riding four-horse chariots and combats between wild or fantastic animals perhaps derive from Anatolia via Greece and then Tarentum or Etruria; and the replacement of figural scenes by inanimate friezes (e.g. friezes of weapons) may come from Macedonian roots. On the other hand, it seems evident that the scenes of armed duels may reflect combats which were the origins of the gladiatorial struggles of later centuries.

In the final phase of Lucanian tomb painting (*c.* 330–*c.* 290 BC) painters prefer larger scenes and larger figures; the tomb itself increases in size and becomes a chamber tomb. Whereas in the case of earlier tombs the painter painted the blocks in the studio prior to their insertion in the rock-cut rectangle, now it was possible, because of the room to manoeuvre inside a chamber tomb, to paint directly on the wall of the tomb. The range of the palette broadened to include new colours, but the great innovation is the use of *chiaroscuro* which lent space and substance to the surface of the paintings. The theme of departure, of saying farewell, evidently came from Greece where it had been a popular theme on Athenian grave reliefs for a good eighty years.

Grave Goods

The arrival of the new population made for big changes with respect to grave goods also; whereas in the fifth century moderation had evidently been the order of the day, some tombs are now richly endowed with goods. A male burial was typically accompanied by weapons and armour of various kinds, most usually of Samnite type, by painted vases of which the *krater*, symbol of the banquet and masculine priority is distinctive, and by strigils, a particular emblem of the athletic world and hence in this context also of the integration of Greek education and training into the new society. A female burial was usually accompanied by numerous pieces of jewellery,

XI *Lucanian tomb painting. Charon (helmsman over the Styx), his vessel, his passenger and her maid, above; lamenting woman, child and another woman bringing offerings, bullock for sacrifice and priest with axe, below.*

fibulae (pins for garments) of silver and bronze, bracelets and necklaces of amber, and occasionally by miniature terracotta objects representing fruit, bread, cheeses, and other farm products – all symbolic of the woman's world. Likewise, vase shapes which accompany women are the *amphora* (the storage jar), the *hydria* (the water jar) and the *lebes gamikos* (the wedding bowl), all vessels associated either with the home or with marriage. Ostentation was at the front of most minds; not all tombs are alike, in their size or their range of goods; social stratification can be recognized. Numerous tombs, presumably of the poorer citizens, consist of plain sarcophagi accompanied by humbler gifts.

The painted tombs of the fourth century and their grave goods are a firm index of a changed society with changed ideas. The richest of the tombs of the fifth century so far recovered were only sparsely equipped with one or two painted vases and a handful of objects; this seemed to reflect a society given to a democratic system with more equal distribution of the city's wealth. In the fourth century, there is no hesitation to decorate some tombs lavishly or to equip them with numerous and rich gifts. It is as if the Lucanian landowning and farming aristocracy had taken over from the previous dominant class and had introduced new attitudes to death and to the commemoration of the dead. Yet, given the continued use of the Greek sanctuaries, the continued use of Greek institutions (the *bouleuterion*, see Chapter 5) and the survival in the tombs of many Greek notions (strigils-athletics) alongside others newly introduced (style and themes for tomb-painting), the amalgamation of leading Greek families into the new Lucanian upper classes is a more probable explanation. With the arrival of the more grandiose chamber tombs towards the end of the century, of which we have only a few by comparison with the smaller tombs of the mid-century, it may even be possible to see the emergence of a few exceptionally well-endowed families, an oligarchy, and detect the sharpening of the social pyramid.

However that may be, and whatever the new political arrangements, the fourth-century tombs and their paintings present an unequalled galaxy of scenes reflecting social, religious and economic life in the city under Lucanian control. The implications of these paintings have yet to be fully explored.

Alexander the Molossian

The appearance of the large vividly embellished chamber tombs seems to coincide with the single major military and political event of the century. The uncle of Alexander the Great, another Alexander, called the Molossian and king of Epirus, was invited into Italy by the city of Tarentum, ostensibly to protect the Greek cities against indigenous oppressors. Around 335 BC his army pushed forward across the peninsula into central Lucania and arrived beneath the walls of Poseidonia. Here a great battle was fought, the Greeks were victorious, and the Lucanians relaxed their grip on the city. Not for long, however. Alexander died in *c.* 330 BC and the city once again fell under the control of the Lucanians. It is after this brief non-Lucanian interlude that the chamber tomb, as a yet more extravagant burial system, makes its appearance; its arrival at this moment may be entirely coincidental. On the other hand, it may signal the concentration of power in the hands of the few; one might envisage a political situation in which the Greeks and any Lucanians who might have sympathized with Alexander and his regime were dismissed or demoted or worse, and the few Lucanian families who had not fraternized assumed full control.

Vase Painting

If the decoration of tombs is one of the artistic merits of the fourth-century city, another is the painting of vases. South Italian vase painting inherited the traditions of fifth-century Greece. Pottery had been imported from Greece from the earliest days of colonization, and there is ample evidence in Poseidonia of Corinthian pottery and Athenian pottery of the sixth and fifth centuries. These styles of pottery were emulated all over the Greek West, and Poseidonia was no exception. In the fourth century, however, South Italian workshops went their own way in the production of painted pottery; there were many artistic currents at work, but none is more famous than that exemplified by the red-figure Paestan studios. The rate of production from these workshops was phenomenal, and the popularity of the wares was not confined to regions close by; for example, Paestan pottery has been found in Campania and in the Aeolian islands.

Two of the major exponents whose names we know from signatures on vases are Assteas and Python; Greeks by name, as we have seen, they wrote in Greek on their vessels, and they used Greek mythological and tragic themes as the subjects of the decoration of their pots. Vase shapes come from the Greek vocabulary: the *hydria* (the water jar), the *krater* (the mixing bowl), the *lekane* (a lidded dish or plate), the *lekythos* (oil or perfume flask), the *amphora* (storage jar). Scenes depicted derive both from the repertory of Greek tragedy and from the contemporary colonial comic theatre which typically highlighted tubby, grotesque, scantily clad male actors prancing about on the wooden stage. Vaudeville and high theatre side by side.

On a *lekythos* in the Paestum Museum, Assteas depicts a scene from classical tragedy: Orestes, Apollo, Artemis and the Erinyes in the sanctuary at Delphi. Protagonists are identified by Greek inscriptions, and the figure style is unmistakably in the Greek tradition: Paestan innovations are the rows of white dots which pick out the hems of garments, belts, bootstraps, and baldrics. Also in the Paestum Museum is the *amphora* of Assteas' contemporary, Python, the principal scene of which shows the birth of Helen. Here the mood is different from the sombre atmosphere of Assteas' Orestes contemplating the bloody dagger. Helen emerges from a large white

Fourth-century Red-figure Vases

66 (above) *Paestan* lekane, *third quarter of the fourth century* BC. *Vases produced in the Lucanian city continued to use shapes drawn from the Greek repertoire, and decorative motifs followed suit. Painters had Greek names and signed themselves in Greek letters. This example is shown upside down so that the figures may be seen more clearly.*

67 (left) *Lekythos by Assteas, third quarter of the fourth century* BC. *Assteas and Python are the two best known artists of the vase painting workshops in Paestum. Here Assteas chose a theme from Greek tragedy: Orestes, Apollo and Artemis at Delphi.*

68 (far left) Paestan red-figure lebes gamikos. Ornate wedding bowls like this are often found in women's graves of the later fourth century. The scene shows Aphrodite and Dionysos; the vase is attributed to Python, one of the best known of Paestum's vase painters.

69 (left) Amphora by Python, third quarter of the fourth century BC. Tongue in cheek, Python portrays the birth of Helen from the egg, which takes centre stage, emphasizing the astonishment of the onlookers rather than Helen's dread fate. Note the signature prominently displayed on the base of the altar.

70 Phlyax vase, mid fourth century BC. A phlyax was a comic actor equipped with mask and padded garments, very popular in fourth-century Italy. The scene depicts an incident from burlesque theatre.

egg which takes pride of place. The egg is placed on an altar while bystanders look on with expressions and gestures of wonderment and surprise; divinities portrayed above smile in amusement and seem more prone to burst into laughter than cognizant of Helen's destiny and the fate of Troy. A master of irony, Python signs prominently on the plinth below the altar. The third great pot-painter in Paestum in these years favours scenes with Aphrodite – an *oinochoe* (wine jug) with the Judgment of Paris, and an *amphora* with the epiphany of the goddess – and hence, since he has not left his signature (or none has survived), he is known as the Aphrodite Painter. This trio of artists painted in the years astride the middle of the century with the larger part of their work completed in the third quarter.

Lucanian Poseidonia used to be thought of as a city in decline; nothing could be further from the truth, as the archaeological record has now revealed. True, there were no more large-scale building programmes, sacred or profane, to match the huge Greek temples of the preceding centuries. But the city did not wither; the barbarians had not arrived. The number and distribution of rural cemeteries shows that agricultural land was worked as never before; populations evidently amalgamated and expanded; the council chamber continued its democratic function; Greek sanctuaries and shrines were respected; painters produced elaborate tomb frescoes of unequalled splendour clearly drawing on Lucanian sources of inspiration; and other painters exemplified the last flowering of Greek vase painting with a style at once elegant and baroque. Poseidonia flourished.

CHAPTER SEVEN

ROMAN PAESTUM

The Colony

The southward march of expanding Rome reached the river Sele and
Poseidonia early in the third century. North of the Sele the prosperous city
at Pontecagnano was destroyed, and the inhabitants replaced by newcomers,
the Picentini, imported from Picenum. South of the Sele a Latin colony was
planted at Poseidonia in 273 BC and the city's name was changed to Paestum.
The change of name is symptomatic of a complete break with the past. The
new colonists took possession of the land: villas replaced the small rural
settlements of the Lucanian period. Though sanctuaries remained largely
intact within the city, the town plan was otherwise radically altered: a
majestic Forum was laid out in the heart of the city. It was situated on a
separate site from that of the Greek agora between the two major sanctuaries
and embellished with characteristically Roman public buildings. Burial
customs changed: cremation replaced inhumation as the preferred method,
with the ashes of the dead buried in urns placed in small rectangular tombs.
Poseidonia ceased to exist: Paestum was born.

Paestum ranged herself politically and diplomatically alongside Rome. She
was a Latin colony, and a coastal one at that; as such, she was expected to
provide ships and sailors in moments of need. Throughout the Carthaginian
wars – titanic struggles which dominated the military and political history
of the third and second centuries BC – and even when Hannibal himself was
prowling around Campania, delighting in Capua and breathing down the
necks of the Paestans, Paestum remained loyal to Rome. We hear of her
offering gold vessels from the temples to Rome in moments of stress (politely
declined by the Roman senate); on another occasion we are told she furnished
cargo boats laden with corn to the Roman fleet setting out to relieve the
garrison beseiged in Tarentum. For this loyalty Paestum was rewarded with
a certain degree of autonomy: she was allowed the unparalleled privilege of
striking her own coins – a privilege she continued to enjoy down to the time
of the emperor Tiberius. The construction however, of the via Popilia
through the Vallo di Diano (behind and to the east of Paestum) in 133 BC
unhappily cut the town off from the principal route for landborne traffic
southward through the peninsula; and the centralization of seaborne trade

in Puteoli, at the north head of the Bay of Naples, did not help matters. The city's importance had begun to wane. Yet, in the first century BC we read from inscriptions of a Paestan notable, one C. Cocceius Flaccus, who made a career for himself in Bithynia and was elevated to the senate by Julius Caesar, and of well-to-do aristocratic ladies – Mineia, Sabina and Valeria – who made major benefactions, in the best Roman tradition, to the city. For Roman literary folk, however, Paestum was of interest only to the poets and only then in a limited, botanical, way; Ovid, Virgil and Martial write eloquently of the roses of Paestum which flowered twice a year, as they do to this day. In the first century AD the emperor Vespasian, from motives still unclear to us, placed a colony of naval veterans from Syria in the city. As usual at Poseidonia/Paestum, however, we can glean less from the written record than from the archaeology.

The Forum

One of the most characteristically Roman elements in town-planning is the Forum. It was positioned in the very heart of the city on a completely new site: a rectangular piazza, measuring as preserved (the full length is unknown

71 Aerial view of Forum and surrounding buildings. To the north, amphitheatre (at right), comitium, temple, shops and so-called gymnasium (beyond); to the south, shops, curia and macellum.

72 Forum, from the west. Laid out on a completely new site soon after the arrival of the Romans (273 BC), the forum was the administrative, commercial and religious heart of the Roman town.

since, like the amphitheatre to the north, it disappears beneath the modern road) about 55 metres in width and 148 metres in length, it was laid out along the east-west axis of the city, its southwest corner touching the central crossroads of the city. There are two major phases of construction. The planning and installation of the complex took place in the third century directly after the foundation of the colony; rows of shops were built along all three visible sides, of similar dimensions and bulk, two-roomed, obviously following a modular blueprint. This architectural emphasis on economic activity bespeaks a city already prosperous and on easy terms with her Roman masters; the contrast with the sister colony of Cosa, also founded in 273 BC, to the north of Rome, could not be sharper. At Cosa, the colony was not installed in a pre-existing city, but was built from scratch; no shops are to be found on the public square in the early phase, and relations with neighbouring states were strained. The two colonies evidently served different purposes; Cosa served as a deterrent to hostile Etruscans, while Paestum was perhaps the outward manifestation of a peaceful alliance between Lucanian aristocrats and Rome. The second phase of construction in the Forum itself is marked by the elevation of a surrounding portico. This portico ran along all three visible sides, was of the Doric Order and made use of earlier materials in a cannibalistic manner not unknown when speed is of the essence. Capitals vary in size and shape, and some are pared down to fit the overall plan. This embellishment of the Forum took place in the time of the first Roman emperor, Augustus.

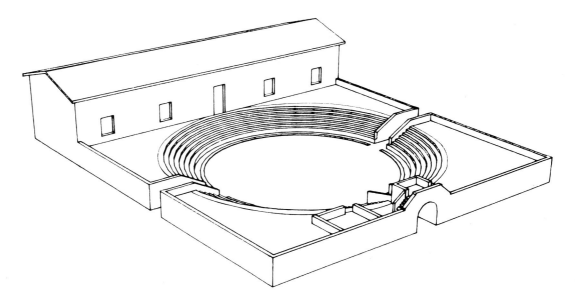

Comitium and Forum Temple

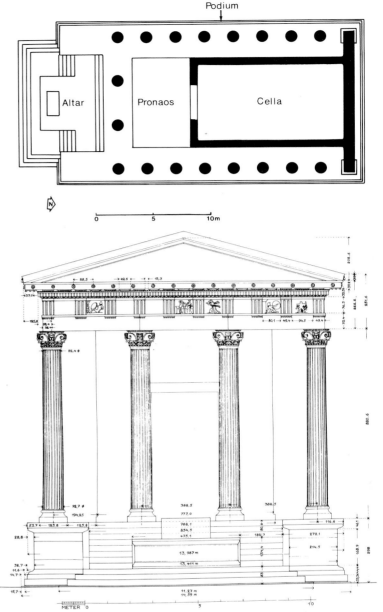

73–78 (opposite above) Comitium, *restored view.* Seats arranged in concentric circles within a rectangular building characterize the place of assembly for the election of magistrates and other political business. (opposite centre) Comitium *as it appears today. View from the northeast with broken columns of the Forum temple at upper right, Temple of Hera II (beyond Forum) at upper left.* (opposite below) *Ruins of the Forum temple from the south, with the Temple of Athena beyond. Raised on a podium and equipped with a frontal staircase – unlike a Greek temple which has flights of steps all the way round – this structure was one of the emphatic signals of the Romanization of Paestum.* (above right) *Plan of the temple. Steps flank the altar at the approach; columns of the Corinthian Order surround three sides of the porch and* cella, *but not the back; the temple is oriented north-south.* (right) *Temple, elevation. Corinthian capitals with huge volutes and female heads support a Doric frieze of triglyphs and metopes in an architectural blending of Orders reminiscent of Greek experimentation three hundred years earlier in the Temple of Athena.* (below) *Forum temple, triglyph and metope. The sculpted metopes depicted running women, drapery flying, or sturdy striding warriors, as here.*

Major public buildings surrounded the Forum. On the north side, perhaps located at the very centre of the north façade, stood an imposing structure: a circular stepped building enclosed within rectangular walls to which passageways gave access from south and east (and possibly originally from the west also), was the *comitium*, the place where public meetings were held for the election of magistrates. The steps were banks of seats; chronologically, the *comitium* was an integral part of the original plan of the Forum. Attached to the *comitium* to the north was the *curia*, the place of assembly for the senate of Paestum; while a small heavily built structure located behind the shops to the northeast and also datable to the earliest years of the colony is identified by some as the *aerarium* (the treasury) by others as the *carcer* (the gaol).

Next to the *comitium* to the west, and indeed violating much of the space and some of the seats of the *comitium* as well as the passageway which originally ran along the west side of the *comitium*, a temple was built. Could these two buildings have ever been in use at the same time? And if the temple was built at a moment when the *comitium* had gone out of use, where is the late republican *comitium*? The temple, originally constructed *c.* 200 BC, was tampered with architecturally on several occasions. Oriented north-south, in sharp contrast to its Greek predecessors and indeed contemporaries (for they were still in use), it is of 'Italic' type. Raised on a high podium and approached by a frontal staircase, not by steps on all sides as is the case with the Greek temples, it stands as a hallmark of the Romanization of the city. A *cella* and *pronaos* were surrounded on three sides by columns of the Corinthian Order (there were none at the back). Corinthian capitals with large volutes, female heads and robust acanthus decoration supported a Doric frieze of triglyphs and metopes; this use of a mixed order (Corinthian and Doric in the same elevation) is typical of South Italian irreverence for architectural rules, and would have brought a wry smile to the faces of Greek architects. The sculpted stone metopes depict warriors and female figures in rapid movement or collapsing postures and evidently derive from Greek prototypes originating from Tarentum. A small altar was raised on a platform which interrupted the steps of the approach from the south. Lively discussion surrounds the identification of this building. It has traditionally been seen as the *capitolium* of the city (the temple of Jupiter, Juno and Minerva, that is). Such *capitolia* typically dominate the fora of Roman towns and were an integral part of the Forum plan. Since, however, there is only a single *cella* (not three – one for each divinity – which would have been expected) and the building was not erected until after the original phase of construction of the Forum, such an identification seems unlikely. If not the *capitolium*, what is it? A new theory proposes that the building be identified as the temple of Bona Mens, a goddess of good sense, moderation, wisdom and memory. Numerous fragments of inscriptions refer to this cult at Paestum, and it has not escaped the notice of any commentator that it is precisely towards the end of the third century BC (after the disastrous defeat at Lake Trasimene at the hands of the Carthaginians in 217 BC) that the cult of Bona Mens was introduced to Rome, and what is more, to the religious heart of the city on the Capitoline. Such a date accords well with the date of the Paestum temple; and if the theory of this temple as the seat of the cult of Bona Mens is right, then the *capitolium* of Paestum may be sought at the unexcavated east end of the Forum.

The temple and *comitium* on the north side of the Forum were matched by two other public buildings approximately in the centre of the south side. Here, the original row of Roman shops was interrupted to accommodate the *macellum*, the public food market, and a basilica. Excavation beneath these buildings has revealed the existence of the remains of a sixth-century temple below, amply documenting the ferocity of Roman planners who did not hesitate, apparently, to infringe on sacred ground when it came to the installation of the new Roman Forum. This area may in the Greek period have formed the northern boundary of the sanctuary of Hera. The *macellum*, rectangular in plan, was provided with four interior marble colonnades from which access was possible to covered shops, and a small shrine facing the entrance: it was built in the second or third century AD. More substantial is the complex adjacent to the west. This building traditionally known as the *curia* (and if so, then a replacement for the earlier *curia* north of the *comitium* on the other side of the Forum) was rectangular in shape and consisted of an open central space surrounded by covered corridors. A large apse-shaped, stonebuilt *exedra* dominated the interior. Recent commentaries suggest that the structure be identified as a basilica, a public building which functioned both as lawcourt and as a place for business deals, rather than as the *curia*. It is dated contemporaneously with the *macellum*, that is to the second or third century AD, and must have replaced another earlier *basilica* which had stood in the same place.

At the west end of the Forum, too, the row of shops is broken to allow the presence of yet another prominent public edifice. This sacred building comprises an oblong *cella* with three rectangular niches against the back wall and a façade which interrupted the portico of the Forum. It is the *Lararium*, the abode of the *Lares*, the divine protectors of the city. Constructed in the form in which it is seen today in the second or third century AD, it stands atop the squared blocks of an earlier building of the republican period which conceivably had served the same purpose. From this western portico of the Forum and from a point close to the central crossroads of the city, came a bronze statue of the satyr Marsyas. The statue was found in five joining fragments; the arms are missing. It consists of a head worked separately, a tubby torso, and stocky booted legs; the workmanship of the head has seemed to some commentators more convincing, more detailed and more expert than that of the body. And this view has led to the supposition that the head may be older than the body, and

79 Bronze statue of the satyr Marsyas, second century BC. Found near the crossroads at the southwest corner of the Forum, this figure, a devotee of Dionysos, stood as an emblem of Libertas, *Liberty*.

80 Amphitheatre, as restored, from the east. Recent stratigraphic investigation has shown that the building was originally constructed in the first century BC, and expanded in the second century AD.

may indeed be reused here from another statue. Yet the disjunction of style may have been deliberate, to suggest the disfigurement of a satyr. According to the myth, Marsyas was rash enough to challenge Apollo to a musical contest which of course he lost; he paid the penalty (death by flaying). Nothing of the Greek myth is suggested in the Paestan Marsyas. Here he may be interpreted ambiguously. First, he stands as a representative of the followers of Dionysos, whose cult was widely appreciated in the third and second centuries BC among native Italic communities, especially those of an anti-Roman bent. Second, he may be seen also as the symbol of *Libertas*, freedom, in which guise he appeared at Rome as well as in the Latin colonies. Both Italic and Roman, then. There is little formally Greek or Hellenistic about this figure; Marsyas is the product of an Italic mentality and of an Italian craftsman.

Forum Dependencies

To the north of the Forum, behind the shops of the north flank, stood two further complexes, each characteristically Roman. At the northeast, the western part of the amphitheatre is visible, with the rest of the building beneath the modern road or further to the east. It was built in two stages. Recent investigation of fills brought in to level the foundations shows that the first phase of construction took place during the first century BC, and that the terraced masonry blocks belong to this first phase. Subsequently, but not before the end of the first century AD, the building was enlarged with the addition of massive brick piers intended to support a further bank of seats. One principal entrance to the arena is situated at the west on the major axis of the structure, while another presumably gave access from the east. Surprising is the modest size of the interior space; surprising too is the location of the building so close to the Forum when Roman amphitheatres tended to be sited – with a wary eye on alien fans – closer to the outskirts of towns. It is worth recalling in this context the pitched battles fought *outside* the amphitheatre at Pompeii between local aficionados and visiting supporters from nearby Nuceria.

At the northwest, again behind the shops of the Forum, but before any block of the amphitheatre was put in place, there was constructed a large complex traditionally known as a Gymnasium. This consists of a huge *piscina*, or swimming pool, with a wide downward ramp leading into it at one end, and a curious amalgamation of built architectural blocks which

*81 Gymnasium-*piscina, *restored view. Originally interpreted as a swimming pool in a gymnasium context, this puzzling complex may now be seen either as a pool used for ritual bathing of the cult statue and followers of the goddess Venus Verticordia, or as a large pool surrounded by trees, a public amenity. Neither recent theory is totally convincing.*

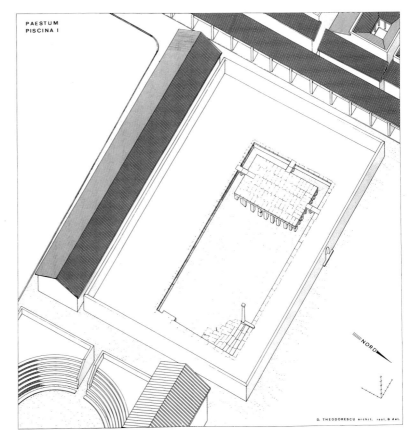

effectively pre-empts much of the interior space at the other. These blocks stood on the floor of the *piscina*, and reached in height to the level of the rim of the pool; when the pool was full of water, they would therefore have been largely, if not entirely, submerged. They have normally been interpreted as supports for a wooden superstructure of some sort. This is the largest structure of its kind from the whole of antiquity, and a recent stratigraphic enquiry has shown that it was built during the third century BC. Can it possibly have been a gymnasium?

Such an interpretation seems unlikely since no parallel exists for such a use of public space in the early years of a colony, nor does the area around the *piscina* provide space adequate for other activities normally associated with gymnasia, i.e. athletics and education. Its use for swimming contests is not plausible, either; such competitions were not favoured in the third century, and much of the interior space of the *piscina* was rendered useless for swimming by the mass of architectural blocks (unless we think of diving boards and diving contests). Nor has any trace survived of grandstands for spectators, though wooden seats and a wooden scaffolding would of course have disappeared. Faced with this conundrum, scholars have recently turned to notices in the literary sources referring to the *piscina publica* at Rome.

The *regio piscinae publicae* at Rome was the zone in which was located the sanctuary of Venus Verticordia; the cult of Venus Verticordia – Venus who turns the heart, from maidenhood to marriage, that is – had merged with that of Fortuna Virilis; and the cult of Fortuna Virilis called for purification and propitiation involving the washing of the cult statue and the immersion of worshippers. It is logical to suppose that such ritual bathing would have taken place in the *piscina publica* (hence perhaps the proximity of the two sites) and equally logical to assume such functions for the enigmatic *piscina* at Paestum. Such an interpretation explains the archaeological difficulties: the ramp at the east could have allowed access to the pool for worshippers descending *en masse* following the bathing of the statue; the architectural blocks at the west could have provided a foundation on which the newly bathed and bedecked statue was placed accompanied by a number of pilgrims or servants of the sanctuary. The area may have been a sanctuary, not a gymnasium; and it may have been the sanctuary of Venus Verticordia/Fortuna Virilis.

On the other hand, there is no sign of a temple, or even a shrine for a statue, which would have been expected if the site had really been a sanctuary. Another theory suggests that it was simply a large public pool, decorated with statues and surrounded perhaps by trees. Yet such an amenity would have been set in a proper piazza, as examples at Pompeii and Herculaneum suggest, which this pool is not; and this theory does not explain the downward ramp or the installations at the west end of the pool. So it remains problematic. It is the size of the pool which is puzzling, and its location so close to the very heart of the Roman city.

The area underwent great changes in the course of the later years of the first century AD. The pool was filled in prior to the eruption of Vesuvius in AD 79 (a stratum of Vesuvian ash was recovered by the excavators), and construction of rooms and porticoes was completed before the end of the century. These units have recently been interpreted as evidence for a *caesareum*, a place for emperor worship; but they are modest by comparison with other Roman *caesarea* and the evidence for such a cult and its priests (the *Augustales*) is hardly extensive. A single inscription referring to the college of the *iuvenes* may refer to a guild centre rather than to the *Augustales*.

Town Plan and Housing

The Forum was incorporated in the new town plan at a point adjacent to and immediately northeast of the major crossroads of the city where the *cardo maximus*, the main north-south thoroughfare and the *decumanus maximus*, the main east-west artery intersected. The Roman planners went about their task in the prescribed and usual way: a grid network of streets was laid out parallel to the two major arteries. West of the *cardo maximus* such a grid arrangement has come to light as a result of excavations while aerial photography reveals its existence elsewhere in the city. A long stretch of the cobbled *cardo maximus*, the so-called Via Sacra, leads from the south gate of the city to the *compitum*, and flanks the sanctuary of Hera to the east. A similar stretch of the *decumanus maximus* leads off from the crossroads towards the west gate, the Porta Marina: in the other direction the eastward run of the *decumanus maximus* is interrupted by the Forum itself, to which access was only allowed on foot, but presumably continued beyond the east end of the Forum to join the east gate. Both these major highways were evidently flanked by porticoes. It seems, from the standpoint of city planning, that public buildings – the Forum and its dependencies, and sanctuaries – cut a wide swathe north-south through the town reaching almost from fortification wall to fortification wall, while private habitations were built on either side. This is certainly true of the area west of the *cardo maximus* where large numbers of private houses have been uncovered; the area to the east of the band of public buildings (i.e. east of the modern roadway) remains in private hands and has not yet been investigated.

Houses are arranged in rectangular blocks separated by smaller streets (*cardines minores*) at intervals of about 35 metres; the shorter sides of the blocks face on the principal street, with the longer on the narrower (at any rate in the southwest quarter where the situation is most legible) and the blocks themselves measure *c.* 35 × 273 m. The blocklike arrangement echoes the plan of Greek cities of the fifth century BC, and may reflect the original city plan of Poseidonia; but the orientation of the Greek temples is at odds with the plan as we know it to have been in the Roman period (see Chapter 2), and the problem of the original design and layout of the Greek city is still unsolved. Given, however, the dogmatic placement and articulation of the Forum, it seems perhaps in character for Roman planners to have insisted on new compass bearings which ignored the alignment of the Greek city gates.

House plans for the most part follow commonplace arrangements such as are found at Pompeii nearby; the *atrium* and peristyle plan is popular, being roomy and airy. The entrance to the house led through a vestibule to the *atrium*, a rectangular court with rooms on all four sides. These rooms were roofed, but an opening to the sky was left in the centre to allow for the circulation of air and for the arrival of rainwater which was collected in a basin, the *impluvium*. The principal room of the *atrium*, the *tablinum*, often faced the entrance way. Behind the *atrium* stood the peristyle: this was another rectangular court, with columns on all four sides in front of rooms, a walkway between the rooms and the columns, and the central area again open to the heavens; sometimes it was furnished with a garden, a *viridarium*. The main room here was the *triclinium*, a dining room. This house plan, which called for high walls and minimal windows (air and light came in from above), seems to our eyes essentially inward looking and somewhat unwelcoming.

Remains of staircases suggest that some houses at Paestum had upper rooms. Little evidence has been found of wallpaintings, and what has survived (or been found thus far) has been monochrome, with red seemingly in particular favour; floor mosaics display geometric patterns of occasionally figured designs in black-and-white or abstract vegetal motifs. By comparison with Pompeii, the houses seem poor. Volcanic debris from the explosion of Vesuvius in AD 79 has been found all over the city, and in some quarters buildings collapsed and were never reused, but for the most part Paestum dusted herself off and life resumed. This means of course that the houses, for the most part originally built in the Roman Republican period, underwent several, if not numerous, facelifts and the richness of wall decoration and furniture found at Pompeii, encapsulated in the Vesuvian debris, could not be expected at Paestum. Some structures, although contained within the block arrangement, show unusual features; striking is one building which incorporates a vast *piscina*, a kind of reservoir perhaps, which takes up the whole width of the city block. Built in the early imperial period, this *piscina* complex was later filled in and replaced by an *impluvium* and a surrounding brickbuilt colonnade. The size of this ambitious installation has led to the theory that we deal here with a clubhouse or the headquarters of some other association rather than with a private residence. Many houses survived until the fourth century AD; some, alas, abandoned their original functions as the city contracted and fell into disrepair, and were converted into limekilns for the burning of the statuary of bygone days.

Attention was paid to the city walls. The precise chronology of their construction remains insecure (see Chapter 5), though it is obvious that various phases are represented, and it seems common sense that they would have been planned very early in the city's life. Yet, a new theory proposes that the whole of the eastern part of the city, and hence the east wall, is an addition of Roman times. The importance to the Romans of the approach from the sea is underlined by modifications to the Porta Marina; here, guard houses were built flanking a courtyard between the external and internal gates, making the entrance to the city from the seaward side yet more monumental. It is likely that the work on both these gates took place in the early years of the colony's life, i.e. still in the third century BC. Some of the towers of the wall were elaborated with capitals and Doric friezes which followed prototypes in the Hellenistic world (such as Pergamum) and which find parallels in towers at Pompeii; these towers may represent Roman work of the second or first centuries BC.

Sanctuaries and Cemeteries

Life in the sanctuaries within the city continued with few modifications: a strip of land at the northern edge of the sanctuary of Hera was evidently appropriated to accommodate the Forum; and the altar of the temple of Hera II was taken down to be replaced by a smaller version and by an avenue of small altars leading northward toward the Forum. Hera remained the major focus of worship (or rather Juno, as she now became) but other votive figurines testify to honours given to Cybele, the Asiatic goddess descendant of the great Mother Goddesses of prehistoric times, and to her lover Attis. A particularly rich haul of votives from the small Italic temple at the northern edge of the sanctuary, perhaps dismantled to make way for the Forum and its dependencies – though the precise chronology of the building is as yet insecure – is thought to have been dedicated to Hera/Juno at the very outset of the colony's life: it includes terracotta babes in swaddling clothes, pregnant women, women with new-born infants, and numerous anatomical votives – eyes, feet, wombs, phalloi, all redolent of a cult devoted to health and fertility. In the sanctuary to the north, Athena remained in charge, now called Menerva (Minerva) as an inscription tells us: the Greek goddess of intellect and warlike protective powers became, it seems, for the Romans yet more potent as she took her place alongside Jupiter and Juno in the Capitoline Triad. Evidence from this sanctuary speaks also of the worship of Aphrodite in the third and succeeding centuries: votive terracottas retrieved include nude female figures resembling Hellenistic Aphrodite types, Erotes, doves, dancers, hermaphrodites, and representations of Dionysos. This has led some scholars to postulate the existence of a temple to Aphrodite in this sanctuary: while there is no evidence at all for such a building, it is clear that worship of Aphrodite/Venus in some aspect took place here in Roman times.

Little evidence has come to light bearing on Roman burial customs – at

82 Terracotta infant in swaddling clothes, early third century BC. New types of votives appear at about the time of the arrival of the Romans; many are concerned with childbirth, fertility and health. See also ill. 83.

83 Terracotta group: mother, child, bathtub, early third century BC.

any rate of the Republican period. There is a surprising and disappointing gap here between the rich panoply of painted tombs of the Lucanian period, and the more humdrum graves used after the turn of the era. All is not entirely lost: in the third century BC it seems that cremation was practised – to judge from a handful of tombs in the *località* Spinazzo – with the ashes of the deceased placed in an urn deposited in a tomb in the shape of a miniature temple. A similar arrangement may be seen in a couple of tombs in the *località* Gaudo. For the second and first centuries BC we are so far in the dark, and when the veil is lifted with the recovery of tombs of the first century AD, customs have changed. Now inhumation is preferred, with the dead interred in graves cut directly in the rock or marked out by rows of bricks or, pathetically, by broken tiles. The grave was sometimes covered with tiles, angled upward and leaning against one another to form a gabled end, a form of burial known at Poseidonia/Paestum since the sixth century BC. Grave goods seem always to be the same in a funeral rite insisting on equality of wealth and status: a lamp, a small pitcher, a bronze coin and a glass *unguentarium* (ointment flask). Occasionally, a female tomb may be distinguished by an unimpressive piece of jewellery, while a few graves have yielded quantities of iron nails preserving still, apparently, the shape of the military sandals from which they came; the prerogative of some soldiers, then, was to have their footgear with them. Tombstone inscriptions of later years recovered sporadically years ago tell us of the careers of individuals whose lives they commemorate and attest to the presence of Easterners in Paestum in the third and fourth centuries AD: thus *Artemidorus* sets up a gravestone for his dead wife, *Zoe*.

The picture of Roman funerary rites in the Paestum region has recently been advanced by new excavations at S. Marco di Castellabate, a site which marks the very southern end of the Gulf of Salerno some 12.5 miles (20 km) from Paestum itself. Here a large Roman necropolis of the first and second centuries AD has been explored: burials vary considerably in size and materials, but grave goods are as consistently banal as those at Paestum herself. Some of the dead were buried directly in the earth, with no covering whatever. Others were covered with layers of stones, and then with terracotta tiles arranged in gable shape; through the ridge presented by the tiles, a terracotta tube was sometimes punched to allow repeated libations to the dead. Other graves displayed a *cocciopesto* (a kind of cement) and stucco covering, punctuated with niches for funerary inscriptions, over the stones which concealed the corpse. Children and infants were buried in large *amphorae*; and occasionally large sherds of large *amphorae* and *pithoi* (also storage jars) were even used to cover adult burials. A very large percentage of these burials are inhumations; two cremation burials are exceptional. The funerary inscription of one speaks of the tomb of Antonia Prisca dedicated by her husband, a *trierarchus* (captain of a ship), and reminds us of the colony of naval veterans planted by the emperor Vespasian. The other preserved the remains of the funeral pyre within the tomb itself – much carbonized pine wood and pinecones. Grave goods whether in inhumation or cremation burials are similar: the by now familiar pitcher, lamp, coin and *unguentarium*, with occasional articles of more personal accoutrement, a bone hairpin, or – very rarely – a gold earring. What kind of settlement these burials belonged to is unclear. However, on the small island opposite S. Marco the remains of a large Roman maritime complex are visible, while at least one farm of the republican period has been found between S. Marco and Agropoli, and sandstone quarries have also been located.

Graves and houses give us a social and economic picture which is entirely coherent. Houses display modest decorative elements (wallpaintings and floor mosaics); few items of furniture have survived with the notable exception of *trapezephoroi*, sculptured stone table supports decorated with lions' paw feet and writhing vegetal motifs. Evidence of sculptural production or consumption is limited with statuary following the common Roman practice of working heads and busts separately so that the off-the-peg busts could be matched with individual heads, and heads could be changed about at will. A glimpse of a more luxurious and challenging world is provided by the gold and ivory miniature group representing Athena and Encelados: a helmeted Athena, spear in hand, darts forward, drapery flying, to dispatch the kneeling giant before her. Posture and gesture, and style of anatomy and drapery are entirely classical in this Hellenistic (early Roman, that is) reprise of the great Greek metaphor for civilization's victory. In spite of this signal of a richer world and of epigraphic evidence (see next chapter) of a few wealthy individuals who made important dedications to the city, it seems that Paestans led lives unencumbered by great possessions in a city declining in importance and becoming a bit of a backwater. The halcyon days of Greek Poseidonia were long gone.

CHAPTER EIGHT

THE SANCTUARY AT SANTA VENERA

Excavation and Setting

As long ago as 1830 terracotta figurines were being recovered from the *località* Santa Venera, directly outside the south wall of the city and some 450 metres east of the south gate. From here too in 1907 came the sixth-century BC sculpted stone metope depicting Europa and the Bull, now in the Naples Museum: since this is the only sculpted metope from the whole of the city of Poseidonia, its lonely presence makes the abundance of sculpted metopes from the sanctuary at Foce del Sele (see Chapter 4) the more emphatic. Evidently, then, by the time of the construction of an industrial works on the site in 1908, it was known that the site was rich in antiquities. The gastronomic landmark then erected was for the manufacture of tomato paste, the famous Cirio brand (hence, the Cirio factory) and Paestum thus in the early years of this century embarked upon a new enterprise.

It flourished, and when an extension to the factory was mooted after World War II, the Superintendent of Antiquities of the day, Pellegrino Sestieri, was moved to undertake excavations in the zone immediately to the east. This he did in 1952. He reported briefly on his work in the *Fasti* for 1953, and published a photograph of the major building he uncovered, which he termed a *heroon* (site of a hero cult) and we term an *oikos* (rectangular religious building without columns and with a single entrance). Sestieri's excavations retrieved fragments of many female terracotta figurines of which his report emphasizes those of archaic date, while storage trays in the Paestum Museum show that he pulled out examples of Hellenistic and Roman date too. He also found fragments of archaic architectural terracottas, and of sandstone archaic Doric capitals and column drums. He proposed that his excavation had revealed an extramural sanctuary, and that this was perhaps dedicated to Aphrodite; he arrived at this tentative conclusion on the evidence of a half-draped female marble statuette and of a damaged inscription which refers to the reconstruction of a temple of a goddess. Although by today's standards his work appears to have been too rapid and no full report was ever published, he was close to the mark. The extension to the factory was built in 1958, and more antiquities were recovered; this new wing was added to the south of the original (1908) factory, fronting the modern road, and to the west of the site of Sestieri's work. More work was done by another Superintendent of Antiquities, Mario Napoli, on the site in the early 1970s, but no report of these efforts has appeared in print.

It is against this background that the Soprintendenza of Salerno, Avellino and Benevento, in collaboration with the Kelsey Museum of Archaeology of the University of Michigan and the Institute of Archaeology of the University of Perugia resumed work in the autumn of 1981. A number of reasons were at the front of our minds. First, in spite of the efforts of Sestieri and Napoli, the identity of the divinity or divinities worshipped remained undetermined. Second, the architectural and cultic history was still largely unknown. Third, the materials found in earlier excavations and kept in the Paestum Museum suggested that the sanctuary had seen continuous use from the sixth century BC down to the third century AD, and offered the possibility that the origins of an important Roman cult might be revealed. Fourth, the large size and the dramatic location of the sanctuary suggested that this was a major state cult. Fifth, the reinterpretation of a fragmentary inscription allowed the conjecture that in the Roman period the deity worshipped was Bona Dea, a mystery goddess about whom little is known. Moreover, the detailed enquiry into architectural and artistic forms, and the imagery used in the sanctuary, would shed light on patterns of cultural influence and exchange where Greeks, and then Romans, mingled with indigenous peoples and with one another. It would also yield evidence on connections between extramural and intramural sanctuaries, and between Paestum and other sanctuaries in the region, those urban and those rural. The work would thus contribute to our knowledge of social and cultural exchange in South Italy in antiquity, and to our knowledge of the process of transmission.

84 Località *Santa Venera, sanctuary site and Cirio factory from the south city wall. Proximity to the city, and size of the sanctuary bespeak the presence of a major state cult.*

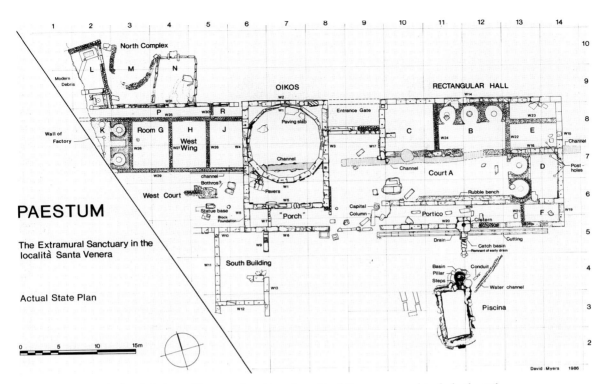

85 Sanctuary in the località *Santa Venera, plan. Remains of buildings preserved include the* Oikos *(temple), Rectangular Hall (for dining ?),* piscina *(pool) with the subsidiary South Building and West Wing. The Cirio factory evidently sits on part of the sanctuary.*

Full-scale seasons of excavation took place in the spring/summers of 1982, 1983 and 1984, and preliminary reports of the results of that work have appeared in the *American Journal of Archaeology*. A study season with a minor amount of excavation took place in 1985, and the preparation of the final publication is now in hand: the first volume which deals with the stratigraphy, the geology, the architecture, the sculpture in stone, the inscriptions, the coins, the metals and the small finds is now in press.

The full extent of the sanctuary is unknown since it disappears infuriatingly beneath the east wall of the Cirio factory: as excavated, it measures some 55 metres east-west by some 37 metres north-south. Entrance was from the north, the direction of the city, and through a gateway between the two major buildings, the Oikos and the Rectangular Hall. These principal buildings, with their highly unusual architectural forms (the circle of faceted blocks in the Oikos; the series of horseshoe-shaped niches in the Rectangular Hall), surely devoted to important cultic activity, are matched to the south by a *piscina*, a fishpond, and the South Building, while a suite of rooms and a courtyard run off to the west. All these buildings would have been visible in the early years of the first century AD after a complex programme of restoration of the sanctuary, funded and promoted by two aristocratic women, perhaps priestesses of the cult, called Sabina and Valeria, had been completed. It did not however begin quite like that.

To the north and between the sanctuary and the city wall there flowed, at certain times, a branch of the river Salso, as a bridge which carried the road over the stream directly outside the south gate of the city amply testifies. The course of this stream from its source, the Capodifiume (and this name seems interchangeable with Salso as the name of the stream itself), beneath the hills of Capaccio to the east, is difficult to trace, though it will have naturally followed the slope of the terrain towards the sea. The Paestans made heroic efforts to control these waters, digging ditches and directing the spring waters around the city walls. Yet it appears that it was too much for them in the end, perhaps because the springwater appeared unpredictably at other parts of the plain than at Capodifiume, bursting forth and careering this way and that, and perhaps because the various creeks or streams it formed rapidly became blocked. By the time of the learned geographer Strabo (first century BC/AD) the region was marshy and had an unenviable reputation as a hot spot for disease; Thomas Major who published drawings of the temples in the eighteenth century describes the Salso by the south wall of the city as 'a rivulet of petrifying water', while Rizzi-Zannoni's plan, similarly eighteenth century, shows aqueducts built to control the waters. In the nineteenth century the distinguished French scholar Lenormant describes the area as abandoned, and the locals as having fled to the hills for fear of malaria. So, these waters, highly advantageous for agriculture, being non-saline, were hard to manage and were undoubtedly one of the factors which contributed to the ultimate decline of the city. They were amply present in the *località* Santa Venera. To the south and east of the sanctuary a large field, liberally peppered with sherds of both Greek and Roman manufacture, is under cultivation and has not been archaeologically explored; some 370 metres away to the south, beyond this field, a large necropolis belonging to the fifth-century BC city has been the subject of recent detailed examination by officers of the Superintendency. Between the city wall, then, and a major cemetery of the Greek city, our sanctuary is located in a suitably prestigious and significant spot.

The first builders of the Oikos and the Rectangular Hall may have had qualms. The site was low-lying, liable to inundation by the vigorous waters of the Salso nearby, and with a travertine shelf or crust (see Chapter 2) very close to the surface. Their first task was to ensure the drainage of the site; to this end they dug long channels in the travertine where the buildings were to rise. Excavation has revealed these channels: beneath the Oikos the channel runs from the line of the east wall westward and was traced for some 7 metres beyond the west wall, while a similar channel runs clear beneath the Rectangular Hall from outside the W wall to outside the E.

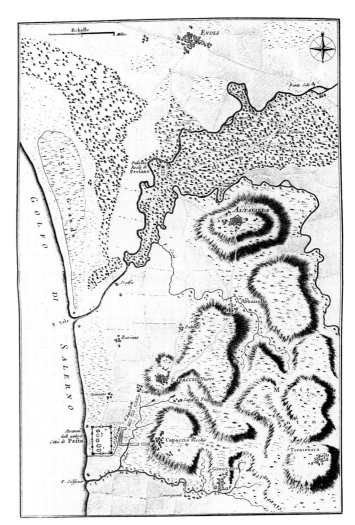

86 Paestum and its environs: engraving of a drawing by Rizzi-Zannoni, eighteenth century. Eboli and the river Sele appear to the north with Albanella, the two Capaccios and Paestum to the south; though the city walls are schematically rendered, the principal buildings are shown as well as aqueducts useful both for irrigation and drainage.

These channels, varying in width between 75 and 120 cm and in depth between 60 and 75 cm, were filled with chips of travertine rubble and showed no sign of stratigraphic accumulation: pottery was all early with nothing later than Archaic Greek. Evidently, the channels were filled with debris at one and the same time. These conduits provided soakaways for drainage purposes, and such trenches are still used to this day by local farmers wishing to drain their land. The Greek builders displayed even more sophisticated techniques: they took care to strip off the upper surface of the travertine crust (which had become impermeable through secondary cementation) to expose more permeable rock and thus facilitate drainage. These tricks of the trade speak eloquently of the building and hydrological skills of the Greek planners; they also provide good evidence of the co-ordinated planning of a major urban complex in the early years of the fifth century BC; and they show that in their first manifestations the Oikos and the Rectangular Hall were virtually contemporary.

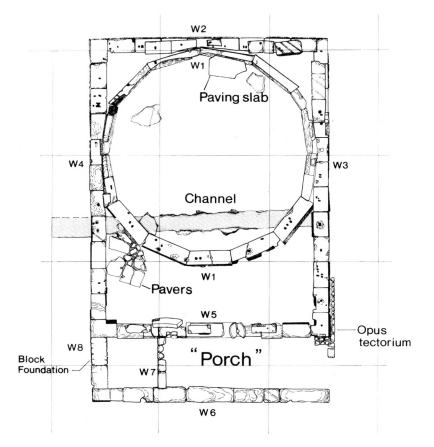

W2

W1

Paving slab

W4

W3

Channel

W1

Pavers

W5

Opus
tectorium

W8

"Porch"

Block
Foundation

W7

W6

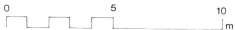

0   5   10
                              m

87 (above) Oikos plan. Oriented north-south, the building offered a large cella *with intriguing interior circle of faceted blocks, and a porch entrance to which was from the east.*

88 Plan of the so-called Heroon at Olympia. The plan of a circle in a square is rare in Greek architecture, so this example provides an important parallel for the Santa Venera oikos.

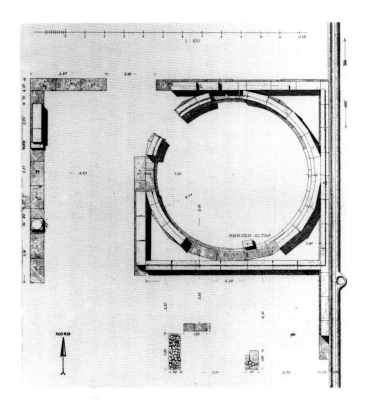

134

89 Oikos, *as viewed from the south. The small Porch is in the foreground, the* cella *with its circle-within-a-square plan, immediately behind it. The roofed tower in the background indicates the line of the city wall, and hence the proximity of the sanctuary to it.*

90 Oikos, *from the southwest. The layout of the* cella, *the larger of the two chambers is clearly visible. Three of the chamber's four walls are in contact with the blocks forming a large circle within the space.*

The Oikos

The Oikos is oriented north-south, and the plan makes use of two rectangular spaces: the larger, the *cella*, is unusual for the faceted circle of blocks in the interior touching three of the four sides, while the smaller formed the 'porch' (actually an anteroom or vestibule or corridor) to the south. Foundations are of rubble, close-packed, while the walls themselves, surviving for the most part as a single course of masonry though with blocks of a second course still *in situ* here and there, are built of rectangular ashlars. These ashlars were quarried from the local tufa (travertine) crusts, are neatly trimmed and dry jointed; the stucco was applied to the exterior.

At first glance, the plan suggests that a single surviving course of blocks at the front (W6 = Wall 6) might have been a stylobate to offer perhaps a tetrastyle prostyle façade. Yet no cuttings may be seen in the upper surfaces of these blocks to accommodate column drums; and though a series of fragmentary sandstone drums come from the site, they were found in various locations, had probably been moved by Sestieri's or Napoli's men, and cannot logically be associated with W6. The foundations of all the walls are contemporary, and the inescapable conclusion is that the south flank of the building was a plain wall. No foundation existed between the southeast corner of the *cella* and the east end of W6; no wall therefore was intended here. This was the entrance to the building. The 'porch' functioned as an anteroom to which access was made from the east. The pilgrim to the sanctuary left the city by the south gate, walked southeastward for some 500 metres, and entered the sanctuary through the north gateway: he or she then turned right into the anteroom of the Oikos, and right again into the *cella*. Such a lateral entrance to the building, and roundabout approach to the circle at its heart would have been entirely consonant with the mysterious activities within.

The construction technique of ashlar blocks on rubble foundations is the same throughout the building, with the sole exception of W7, a late intrusion which sported no foundation whatever. Small patches of a *battuto* – crushed limestone, thin and powdery, rolled flat – floor belonging to the building in its first phase have been recovered; but the floor has largely vanished in the face of extensive Roman remodelling (the paving slab visible at the north belongs to the final phase of the building's life). Important Greek buildings at Poseidonia were normally provided with ashlar foundations, while the combination of rubble foundations supporting walls of ashlars does not seem to appear before the third century. Yet rubble foundations provide handsome drainage opportunities, and in other areas, where there was a danger of flooding – the sanctuary of the Kabirioi at Thebes, for example – Greek builders of the fifth century BC used rubble foundations. Such a use here chimes well with the evidence of the channel dug in the travertine before building began.

91 Rim of Athenian black-figure plate by the Polos Painter, second quarter sixth century BC. Sherds like this can be ready pointers to the age of the stratum in which they are found (they give a terminus post quem = *date after which). They also provide evidence of trading activities between Poseidonia and Athens (or Athenian outlets).*

The proportions of the building are consonant with the practices of Greek builders at the end of the archaic period, the unit of measurement employed is a foot of 0.347 m (comparable with a Greek foot of 0.351 m used for the first Temple of Hera and another of 0.343 m used for the Underground Shrine), and archaeological materials retrieved from the foundations suggest a construction date of *c.* 490 BC. There are many hundreds of chronologically identifiable sherds – fragments of imported Corinthian and Attic wares provide the most familiar and friendly markers – and only a single sherd, a rim fragment of a coarse ware cooking pot, which *may* be later; yet, if later, it is puzzling that it is the only example found, since more later material would have been expected. The presence of this baffling sherd, if it is later, is best explained in the context of (Roman) disturbance and contamination. The same may be said of the only other intruder. This is a bronze coin, a Paestum issue of the late third-early second century BC, unearthed in foundation materials associated with W3. Again, no other material from the *locus* (the stratigraphic unit) in which the coin was found, or in associated *loci*, is to be dated later than the early fifth century; again, upper levels yield evidence of Roman activity; again, if the coin were to be a true index of date of construction, then later fifth-, fourth- and third-century pottery should have appeared in these *loci*: the chronological gap between the other materials and the coin is too large to be explained otherwise than by intrusion caused by Roman repair work. All the evidence, then – the construction technique, the proportions, the unit of measurement, and the materials from the foundation – is at home in the Greek world of the fifth century BC. The plan of a circle within a square is uncommon in Greek architecture, and very rare in a sanctuary context: a significant parallel however to the Paestan Oikos is to be found at Olympia. A building just outside the west wall of

92 Votive miniature kraters. *Groups of votive miniature pots like these were deposited in foundation materials for significant repairs to the building; in this instance beneath a new floor associated with the refurbishment of the front part of the structure.*

the Altis, excavated and published as a *heroon,* shows similar features. Though different in dimensions and in the provision of a colonnaded façade, it is similar in concept and in the scale of the circle in the interior. This building too has been dated to the fifth century BC.

The foundations of the exterior walls are bedded right down on the travertine shelf while those of the faceted circle on the inside are less substantial and do not always reach the travertine. The obvious implication is that the exterior walls were loadbearing, while the circle was not; this view is supported by the evidence of the blocks of the circle to the north, ashlars turned on their sides, so to speak, thin and improbable supports for further masonry. Of the elevation, then, it is clear that the circle was not intended to be seen from outside the building, and that the Oikos would have appeared as a rectangular structure. It seems that the semicircle of blocks to the north of the circle functioned only as a screen, while those to the south may have taken a second course of masonry (pryholes in surfaces support this). The upper part of the walls of the fifth century building was probably built of timber and mudbrick; and painted architectural terracottas would have decorated the roof.

Compelling evidence has come to light of repairs to this building carried out by the Romans in the second century BC. A rather irregular series of paving slabs (pavers), datable by pottery beneath, bears witness to the installation of a new floor at the front of the *cella*, and this was accompanied by another new floor, a hard thin patchy pavement both inside and outside the 'porch'. This second floor sat on a rubble foundation embedded in which was a group of votive miniature kraters; it is doubtless significant that these votives are placed in the foundation for a new floor close by the entrance to the temple. Immediately outside the building, near the southwest corner of the *cella*, a pit was dug so close to the building that it chopped through the foundations; it was filled with a remarkable haul of fourth century and Hellenistic pottery which included many complete shapes: there are 10 kg of pottery from this pit and an unusually high percentage (45 per cent) is fine wares. This must represent a deposit of previously dedicated objects removed

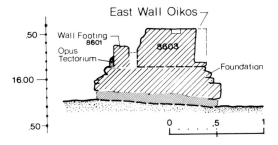

93 Oikos, *section through the east wall showing* opus tectorium (= *stucco work). The ashlars of the wall received a rubble addition on the exterior coated with* cocciopesto (*a hydraulic cement with a liberal admixture of broken or crushed potsherds and lime) and stucco, representing repairs carried out in the first century* BC.

94 (right) *Inscription recording the benefactions of Sabina (line 1) to the sanctuary, first century* BC. Opere tector(io) *(line 4), and* sedes et pavi(menta) *(line 5) are all mentioned. The inscription may be restored to read: 'Sabina, wife of Flaccus, saw to the construction of the goddess' shrine from the ground up, to the decoration with stucco work, and to the provision of seats and pavements; she paid for it with her own money, and she approved the work.'*

to a hallowed spot after temple cleaning, or, better, a refounding deposit. The pottery ranges in date from fourth to mid-second century BC while a single coin found here is the only Republican coin from the whole site, a badly corroded uncial *as* dated 'third-second century BC'; a likely date for the deposit then is mid to late second century. At the point where the pit was cut, the wall of the Oikos consists of a single block with scant foundations; likewise, the southwest corner block has little rubble foundation, allowing the conjecture that the whole corner might have been reworked at this time.

About 100 years later more work was needed on the Oikos. A massive pier of square cut blocks was placed at the southeast corner of the *cella*, evidently intended to strengthen the corner and solidify the northern jamb of the entranceway. Opposite, to the south, the entrance was dignified further by the installation against the exterior of W6 of a rectangular basin, waterproofed on the interior and probably intended for ritual purposes. The east wall (W3) preserves traces of a rubble addition to the exterior; this flimsy broadening of the wall was embellished with *cocciopesto* on the surface towards the bottom of the wall, and with stucco elsewhere. The whole project was evidently planned to brighten up the entrance, and the new rubble wall footing with its accompanying decorative surfaces may be identified with the *opus tectorium* provided for the temple by a certain Sabina. An inscription found at the site records Sabina's benefactions to the

95 *Alabaster* alabastron, *fifth century* BC. *Alabastra were small jars for oil or unguents used in connection with sports. Here a votive offering to the goddess,* alabastra *frequently accompanied male burials in the fifth century as gifts.*

sanctuary: she repaired the temple, she decorated it with *opus tectorium*, she provided seats (*sedes*) and pavements (*pavimenta*), she paid for it all with her own money, and she approved the results of the work. Scraps of the *opus tectorium* have been identified; and the single paving slab preserved within the circle surely represents Sabina's gift – we may suppose that the rest of the circular pavement has disappeared since antiquity (Sestieri's photograph of 1952, however, showed two blocks surviving, so one has vanished since then); no trace of the seats however has come to light, though a single fragment of a marble seat, or a footstool, with the leg terminating in a lion's paw, perhaps deriving from a cult statue, was found in earlier excavations.

First built in the early fifth century BC, the building survived with essentially the same shape and scale until the first century AD. Major repairs to the floors were undertaken in the second century BC and possibly to walls and superstructure also. A wide-ranging project of renewal was taken in hand in the first century BC under the auspices of the indulgent Sabina. The eruption of Vesuvius in AD 79 will have had serious consequences (buildings to the west collapsed) but precise information is lost since earlier excavations removed the upper stratigraphy. Material from pits, however, testifies to some activity in the second and third centuries AD, and to a rather active medieval presence in the thirteenth century.

The layers of earth around and in the Oikos were thickly larded with votive objects of all descriptions: fragments of terracotta figurines, objects of bone, alabaster and amber, loomweights of terracotta and lead, pots and groups of pots. There can be no doubt that the building's function was religious. The numerous complete pyramidal and discoidal weights were a cheap form of dedication to the divinity, and a large concentration of them – no less than forty-seven, in fact – was found in the entrance to the sanctuary. The industrially-minded will be tempted to think of weaving activities – an impossible scenario, however, given the findspot and the fact that the weights were not systematically arranged, when found. They are undoubtedly votives, representative of the *mundus muliebris*, the women's world, and just the thing, cheap and handy, for a gift from a woman to a female deity. Just the thing, too, to dedicate on entering a sacred place.

Terracotta figurines are more ambitious gifts; the new excavations have retrieved upwards of two hundred across the whole site of which many come from the Oikos and its environs. Most are female with one or two intriguing interlopers. The female types include those in common use in Poseidonia (seated figure holding a child, for example), others with very tall headdress imported from Rhodes – these of fifth century BC date – and others including the far-famed Tanagra types of Hellenistic date. Male figures include one lissome character, proud of genitalia and buttocks, large *patera* (bowl) in hand for a generous libation, sombrero on his head. The headgear is reminiscent of Etruscan representations and reminds us that in Greek and

96-98 (above) Female head. The polos (headdress) is a typical
attribute of one of the most popular seated Hera types at
Poseidonia. (below) The high headdress of this female head is
characteristic of figurines made from moulds imported from
Rhodes in the eastern Mediterranean. Rhodians joined in the
foundations of Gela and Acragas in Sicily, and this may suggest
the route by which the type arrived in Poseidonia. (right) Almost
all the votive figurines in the sanctuary are female, but here is an
exception. The bowl held in the crook of the arm signals his
intention to pour a libation; the extravagant hat finds parallels in
the Etruscan world.

99 *Bone cosmetic box in the form of a*
duck, lower part, from a Roman context
but conceivably an heirloom. An item from
the feminine boudoir, this box would have
been a particularly suitable gift for
Aphrodite/Venus.

Lucanian days, Etruscans were nearby just north across the river Sele at
Pontecagnano. Some 70 per cent of figurines found in the new excavations
are of archaic date; yet of about one thousand found by Sestieri and Napoli,
some 65 per cent are fourth century or Roman. Thus, the divinity worshipped
here remained in vogue right down into Roman times, and like the
architecture, the figurines testify to continuity of activity in this hallowed
spot. What the percentages above underscore is neither that the godhead
was more popular in Greek times (new evidence) nor in later periods (old
evidence) but that the earlier excavations stripped off the floors and materials
of the Hellenistic phases, leaving Greek strata (in some areas) to be retrieved
by us: the stratigraphic investigation has confirmed this conclusion. Other
more exotic or personal votives include an amber pendant (amber is well
represented in Poseidonia by the fifth century BC), the lower part of a bone
pyxis (cosmetic box) in the shape of a duck (context is Roman), ivory
hairpins (Roman) and a partially glazed vase in the shape of a phallos. Much
evidence, then, of devout pilgrims making gifts to a favoured deity.

The Oikos with its intriguing interior circle is the most imposing, as well
as the most enigmatic, of the group of impressive and puzzling buildings in
the sanctuary. The entrance to the building is on the flank, the approach to
the *cella* is circuitous, and obviously the most important events took place
within the circle. What were they? The plan of the building is echoed in the
so-called Heroon – site of a hero cult – at Olympia (correctly called a

100 Ivory hairpins, Roman. Objects of women's adornment, these pins made appropriate gifts for a female divinity concerned with the attractiveness of the appearance.

Heroon on the basis of *Hellenistic* inscriptions; but was it a *Heroon* in the fifth century?), where altars found inside the circle specify the use of the area, for sacrifice. Similar evidence comes from an Oikos in a sanctuary complex found at Sabucina in Sicily. Sixth-century BC in date, the rectangular Oikos at Sabucina incorporated segments of an earlier circular structure touching three walls of the interior; a circular altar stood in the centre. This evidence is compelling. Excavation in front of the Paestum Oikos to the south, where an altar might have been expected, has turned up no such structure; it is evident, then, that the altar(s) stood inside the circle. The Oikos was therefore a, if not the, principal temple of the sanctuary, and the interior was used for sacrifice and related ceremony.

The South Building (ill. 85)

Adjacent to the south stood the South Building, for which two chronological phases have been established. The earlier, represented by W11, W12, and W13, is of the Archaic period; construction technique is the same as for the Oikos, and the foundations are noteworthy for the quantities of sherds of

Corinthian wares they have yielded. It is tempting to think of this structure as perhaps the oldest on the site, and yet more tempting (and even more speculative) to link it with a number of archaic architectural members found in earlier excavations (unprovided, alas, with precise findspots). Thirteen badly eroded sandstone column drums (sandstone is normally associated with sixth-century construction at Poseidonia); a large Doric capital endowed with sixth-century profile and dimensions; and the metope depicting Europa and the Bull. These elements suggest the elevation of an important building, and it would be convenient if they belonged together, and there were a suitable stylobate on which to set them. Yet the capital is too large for the drums, and no logical position can be suggested for the metope in the absence of more evidence (architrave or triglyph blocks etc.). Other large Doric capitals are found reused in the third century BC elaboration of the Rectangular Hall, so this capital too may have been reused somehow; and if not reused, it is as likely to have been dedicatory, given its size, as structural. It is just possible, however, since there is nowhere else to put them – unless we fantasize a building lost beneath the Cirio factory; the extent of the sanctuary beneath the factory is currently unknowable – that the column drums could have belonged to this building. The wall lines disappear beneath the Cirio factory and could not be followed, but the implied shape is that of a *stoa*, an architectural form common in Greek sanctuaries: we may perhaps then hypothesize a *stoa* here, oriented north-south and facing east.

The later phase in the South Building is Roman. The redevelopment of the area which began in the first century BC called for repairs to the Oikos and for the linking of the Oikos to the South Building. Thus, the spur wall, W9, was butted up against the south wall of the Oikos and aligned with W13, while the closing wall, W10, was built between the south-west corner of the Oikos and the adjacent corner of the South Building. Accordingly, the west court was created, and an additional space was provided at the northern end of the South Building. The archaeological evidence is, alas, ambiguous. An alternative interpretation suggests that the spur wall, W9, is part of the original *Archaic* complex; and that the South Building was dismantled in, or had disappeared by the time of, the Roman reworking of the area. No evidence exists to permit speculation on the history of the South Building between its first construction in the early fifth century BC and the Roman programme of reconstruction.

The West Wing (ill. 85)

The West Wing consists of a set of rooms (G, H and J) and part of a peristyle court embellished with two horseshoe-shaped spaces forming the east side; these omega-shaped niches parallel almost precisely those to be seen in the Rectangular Hall. The west court lies to the south. The whole

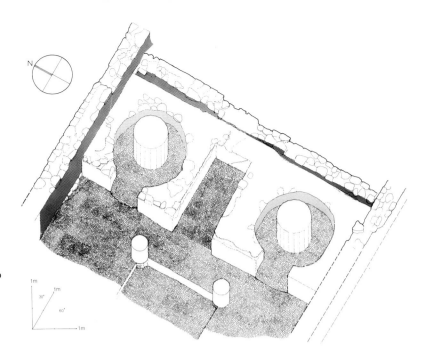

101 West Wing, Court K, axonometric view of niches. Built in the early first century AD and put out of commission by the eruption of Vesuvius in AD 79, the purpose of these niches remains enigmatic.

complex shows the same kind of construction techniques, and all walls were built – to judge from associated pottery – at the same time in the course of the first century BC. Here Roman builders went all the way down to the travertine crust with their foundation fills, and no trace remained of any pre-existing buildings or activities. Two flimsy floors survived in the rooms, the earlier of which was contemporary with the walls, while the later testifies to the use of the area in the second and third centuries AD. There is, however, no trace of a threshold, nor any other indication of how access to these rooms was intended.

More dramatic is the situation in peristyle court K. Here stand two niches, equipped with central reused Doric column drums, and with waterproof *cocciopesto* floors and walls. The floors of the niches are *c.* 15 cm higher than the floor outside the entrance (likewise, of *cocciopesto*) and a smooth

102 West Wing, Court K, omega-shaped niche and column drum, from above. Waterproofed floor, lip at entrance and side of niche prove provision for water to course about – for cleaning purposes? For general amenity? For religious reasons?

sloping surface linked the two floors; a step might have been expected, but the architect provided instead the smooth lip, evidently intended to ease the flow of water. In front of the niches, the floor drops steeply at right angles for *c.* 20 cm, levels off into a second floor and vanishes beneath the Cirio factory. Stuccoed column drums stand at the corners of the lower floor, suggesting that the space between the niches and the lower floor formed part of a peristyle, the balance of which is lost to view beneath the factory. Another column drum found lying on the floor and therefore not *in situ*, doubtless came from another (facing?) niche. It is noteworthy that the space occupied by the West Wing (as hypothesized with a complete court K) is close in size to that to the east of the Oikos; such a balancing of space either side of the central unit would have offered a solution pleasing to a Roman planner.

The more northerly of the two niches in K was cleared by earlier excavators. In 1984 we found the rectangular unit between the niches choked with volcanic ash; preserved to a depth of *c.* 15 cm, this ash sat on the very floor of the building. Similarly, a thick deposit of ash was found on the floor of the southern niche and all around the column drum (depth, *c.* 20 cm). Many fragments of rooftiles came to light here too, evidently representing a collapse of the roof and testifying that this was one building left untidied and never reused. A lamp fragment and a single sherd found here are of the early first century AD, and the whole ensemble reflects the damaging results of the eruption of Vesuvius in AD 79. The floor in front of the niche was chopped through and archaeological materials from beneath gave a *terminus post quem* of the second half of the first century BC. A more exact fix for the date of construction is obtainable from material beneath the floor of unit L; unit L and corridor P both preserved secure stretches of the same *cocciopesto* floor as that in K, and archaeological materials beneath gave a *terminus post quem* of the early first century AD. So, while the walls of G, H, J and K are all contemporaneous and datable to the first century BC, it seems that the *cocciopesto* floor in K and the elaborate niches are an installation of the beginning years of the first century AD. Their function will be discussed in the section dealing with their counterparts in the Rectangular Hall; they are so far without exact parallel in Roman architecture. The floor in P is only preserved at the extreme west end, hard up against the debris piled against the factory wall, and it appears to have been chopped through vigorously by Sestieri's men. Atop the floor there was again much volcanic ash, amidst which again were many fragments of joining rooftiles; while from beneath the floor came a large piece of the stem of a *thymiaterion* (incense burner) of the fourth century BC with the usual Greek dedicatory verb: ANETHEKE (Dedicated).

Two surfaces, hardly floors, appeared in the West Court; they are contemporaneous with the phases in the rooms to the North. With the late republican phase are associated a rectangular boxlike chest, something like

103 Inscribed sherd of black glaze thymiaterion *(incense burner), fourth century* BC. *Found beneath the floor in Corridor P, the incense burner was inscribed in Greek letters* ANETHEKE *(= dedicated), proclaiming the gift of the vessel to the divinity in the fourth or third century.*

a Greek *bothros*, built of upright masonry slabs, and a rectangular well-founded block aligned with the front wall of the *cella* of the Oikos, which probably served as a statue base. With the phase of the imperial period goes an altar. Thus, we can envisage in the Roman period an open-air courtyard equipped with some of the necessary paraphernalia of sanctuary life: an altar, a *bothros* (or *eschara* (a hearth)?) and statuary.

The Rectangular Hall (ill. 104)

The largest building in the sanctuary is the Rectangular Hall, where three phases of building activity may be detected: in the first phase (Greek) an oblong structure rose on the site, of which the exterior walls (W14, W15, W16, W17) are distinguishable. Shortly after the arrival of the Romans, a portico was added along the length of the south flank (phase 2); and in the early first century AD, the whole of the interior of the building was restructured (phase 3), a major component of which was the five omega- or horseshoe-shaped niches and their accompanying reused column drums.

As with the adjacent Oikos, a long channel was dug for drainage purposes, in the travertine crust before the Greek builders began work. Circular postholes discovered by excavators in 1983 and 1984 cut in the crust near the east wall herald the presence of domestic activity in prehistoric times. The Greek builders used the same materials as those used in the *oikos*. The exterior walls are preserved to at least one course of masonry, and a stretch of one interior wall (W18) bisecting the interior and bonded into the east wall was also found. The date for construction, provided by pottery from the foundations, is sometime early in the fifth century BC. A thin *battuto* – crushed and pressed limestone – floor was found associated with the fifth-

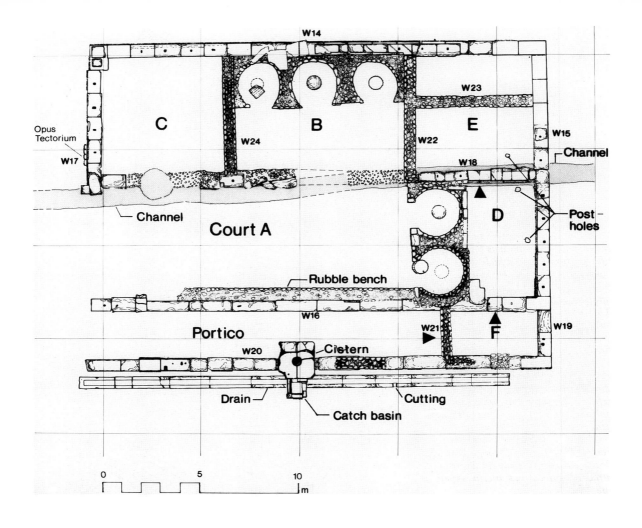

century building in all the (later) rooms of the Hall (Rooms B, C, D, E): this floor puts in only sporadic and patchy appearances since it was seriously disturbed by Roman work. However, a large stretch of it, luckily preserved, though cut to accommodate the later Roman wall, W24, was found in Room C. Here the fifth-century floor had subsided beneath the weight of the heavy rubble foundations for the Roman installations, but remains tidily attached to the fifth-century wall, and had in fact undergone an early repair.

In and beneath the floor there came to light a rich concentration of materials – pottery including intact and completely mendable pots, fragments of terracotta figurines, archaic black glaze lamps, many loomweights, an iron knife, many miniature votive pots, fragments of bronze, iron, lead, alabaster and amber, and many bones and shells. There is evidence of stratigraphic compression here, with the *battuto* floor pressed down into materials originally beneath it, thanks to the weight of the superimposed Roman floor. Moreover, it seems likely that Roman disturbance accounts

Rectangular Hall

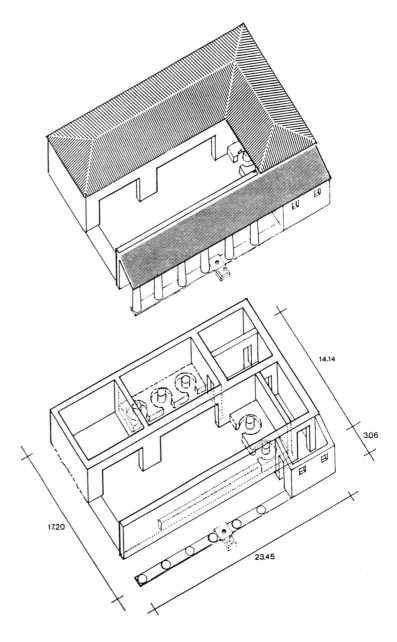

104 (opposite) *Plan. The original rectangular building was built in the fifth century* BC, *to which the colonnaded portico was added in the middle of the third century shortly after the Romans arrived in Paestum. The interior was reworked in its entirety, with provision of the horseshoe-shaped niches, in the early first century* AD.

105 (right) *Axonometric views, showing the building after the refurbishment of the first century* AD: *abbreviated portico, niches installed, central area open to the skies.*

106 (below) *Section through* battuto *floor in Room C, showing floor attached to wall and ancient repair to the floor.*

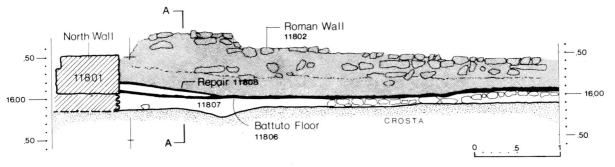

A

North Wall

Roman Wall
11802

.50

11801

Repair 11808

16.00

11807

.50

.50

16.00

.50

A

Battuto Floor
11806

CROSTA

14.14

3.06

17.20

23.45

0 . . . . .5 1

for the appearance cheek by jowl of materials brought in as part of the fill for the underpinning of the Greek floor, and others deposited on or close to the travertine crust as ritual offerings. The quantity of intact pots and votive objects and the excavators' observation that many were deposited in orderly fashion leave no doubt that ritual activity took place here. The materials themselves point illuminatingly to the function of the Hall in the Greek period. The large numbers of animal bones, mostly sheep/goat, speak of sacrificial activity, while the bird bones, with both meat and non-meat bearing bones present, speak of the disposal of whole birds in sacrifice, and the chopping of the bones points to preparation for eating. Ample evidence, then, for sacrifice and dining – hallmarks of sanctuary life.

Entrance to the Hall was from the west, thus emphasizing the east-west axis of the building. Shortly after the Romans arrived, however, they expanded the Hall southward by the addition of a colonnaded portico, thus drawing attention to the south side of the building. The portico was provided with a drain in front to gather rainwater from gutters, with a catchbasin to allow unsavoury sediment to settle, and with a cistern positioned astride and beneath the stylobate. Doric capitals were reused here in energetic and economic Roman manner for the bottom of the catchbasin (upper surface of an *abacus*) and for the head of the cistern (shaved down and bored through). A capital of much smaller proportions and a monolithic column found near the eastern end of the portico and trapped in a more recently formed travertine, allow a reconstruction of the elevation of the south façade with nine columns in this, its original phase. Pottery from foundation levels shows that the portico, cistern, drain and basin were all built sometime shortly after *c.* 275 BC. The new portico was aligned with the front wall of the *oikos* in a Roman systematization which underscored the architectural and religious links between the two structures.

The major revamping of the building concerned the interior when new walls were inserted along with the five omega- or horseshoe-shaped niches. On the façade, the east end of the portico was abbreviated to form Room F. Foundations of all the new walls are of coursed rubblework faced with squared blocks, while the walls themselves, as preserved, continued upward in the same way. The niches were built in similar fashion; and by analogy with their counterparts in the West Wing, they were probably equipped with a stucco dressing on the walls and with *cocciopesto* floors. A thick compact layer of rubble tumble was put down, as deep as 45 cm in parts of Room E, to serve as the underpinning for the niches and for floors in Rooms B, C, D, E; and pottery from the foundations puts the construction firmly in the early years of the first century AD. One of the problems here is the absence of the floor: it is surprising that no trace survives *in situ*. It may be (1) that earlier excavators effectively removed it, or (2) that the floor system used was flimsy and has vanished, or (3) that the building in this phase was never completed. Yet scraps of pavement were found in fill, which seems to

Rectangular Hall

107-109 (above) Votive terracotta loomweights. Weights like these were found in and around both the Rectangular Hall and the Oikos. Cheap and handy dedications, and suitable offerings by women to a female divinity, they have been found in numerous sanctuaries in South Italy and Sicily. (right) Cistern head astride stylobate of portico, from south. In the foreground, remains of an earlier north-south drain; in front of the cistern head and stylobate, a settling basin and channel for collection of rainwater from the eaves en route to the cistern. (below) View of east wall from the west showing postholes cut in the travertine crust to the right, drainage channel beyond, and east-west transverse wall bonded in the east wall.

eradicate options 2 and 3, and the evidence from the West Wing is instructive. At the very western end of Corridor P the tough *cocciopesto* floor was found, disappearing westwards beneath the factory and chopped through irregularly across the width of the corridor; not a whisper of it has survived from the whole of the remainder of the corridor's length. This suggests forcefully enough that it is the earlier excavators who removed the floor of the corridor, and by extension the floors of the Hall.

An inscription found in the sanctuary records that a certain Valeria gave the *[str]ongyla*, a word which in this context is difficult to understand. The word itself, in Greek, is an adjective and means 'rounded' or 'circular'. Here, then, it is neuter plural and means 'rounded things'. Now, other inscriptions referring to dedications refer to buildings or parts of buildings such as pavements or seats; may we then think that the *strongyla* given by Valeria were architectural and may we associate them with the mysterious rounded niches?

What was the function of these niches? The provision of waterproofing for floors and walls (by analogy again with the West Wing) suggests that water was intended to flow around the column drums; this allows the proposal that these units may have been *nymphaea* (elaborate Roman arrangements, making much use of architectural façades, sculpture in niches or standing on bases, and much water flowing about from fountains). Yet the column drums show no trace of cuttings to take tenons for statues, nor does this plan echo that of any known *nymphaeum*. Closest architectural parallels appear in arrangements for seated dining. Roman dining normally entailed couches arranged for people to eat in a reclining position: seated dining was however common in the Greek world in sanctuaries, and there is evidence at Pompeii for such a Roman arrangement – though not in a sanctuary. Certainly the function of the building in the Greek period and the notion of continuity of purpose would support the dining theory. A third suggestion points to the presence of the bench set against the interior of the south wall of the court, evidently intended for seating, and therefore probably for waiting. For what? Other sanctuaries, such as Samothrace, make provision for pilgrims waiting for revelations of mysteries; could the *strongyla* then be places for safekeeping of cultic objects to be revealed to devotees at ritual moments? Column drums could then have supported religious emblems or statuettes, fixed on plinths, and the niches themselves could have been curtained off until the critical moment. Was the Rectangular Hall a Hall of Mysteries?

The Piscina

The area to the south of the Hall had been left untouched by Sestieri and Napoli. In 1982, therefore, we began excavation here, with the intention of recovering an undisturbed section of the stratigraphy of the site. The so-called medieval travertine crust had sealed the whole area, so that progress initially was difficult; what emerged here was a feature somewhat unusual for a sanctuary – a *piscina*, a fishpond. Over the course of four seasons the structure was excavated in its entirety: it measures about 6 × 3 m but is curiously aligned (while the north wall is parallel to the south façade of the Hall, the south wall is not) and approximately rectangular in shape. Built of ashlar blocks backed by earth and stones and topped by horizontally laid slabs, the walls were heavily encrusted on the interior as a result of continuous contact with the calcium rich waters of the Capodifiume. The east and west walls were both pierced by holes, plugged by *amphorae*, proving beyond question that this tank had functioned as a fishpond; such *amphorae* embedded in the walls of ponds are typical features of Roman fishponds and were used by fish or eels as secure places for laying eggs or for shelter from sun, light and heat. A pear-shaped basin was attached to the north side of the pool; access to this basin from the pool was made by means of steps, so that humans (as well as fish) were intended to enter here. In the centre of the basin stands a heavily encrusted mushroom-shaped pillar; removal of the encrustation atop this pillar (which stood to the approximate level of water within) revealed a lead-lined rectangular sinking to take the tenon of a statuette. Two conduits, one of collared terracotta pipes and another open tile-and-mortar channel, provided for the arrival of water into the tank, for the removal of overflow, and for circulation of fresh water. All joints of blocks, pipes or tiles were sealed with the same hydraulic mortar which coated the interior of the pool.

Pottery from fills brought in to buttress the exterior of the *piscina* tells us that the pond was constructed in the early first century AD. Its situation opposite the Hall and pointing towards it, may have been dictated by the dimensions of the abbreviated portico, shortened by the creation of Room F at its eastern end. Its north-south axis is aligned on the midpoint of the newly curtailed portico. Accordingly, Hall and *piscina* were visually linked; the Rectangular Hall, in its redeveloped state, and the *piscina* were part and parcel of an overall first-century AD plan for the sanctuary. Moreover, there are clear formal analogies between the *strongyla* of the Hall and the basin of the fishpond: pear-shape and horseshoe-shape, central column drums and pillar. Furthermore, fishponds of similar size appearing in garden *piscinae* at Pompeii are often surrounded by porticoes; at Paestum the Hall provides the portico, the setting for the pond. In spite of evidence of encrustation on the interior of the pond and of the water conduits, and of the likelihood of repeated episodes of stagnation as a result of the interruption of the water supply, the *piscina* continued in use until the eruption of Vesuvius in AD 79. Ash fall then blocked the conduits; flooding ensued; stagnation and encrustation followed, so that within a short time the pond fell out of use. By the final years of the century systematic filling in of the *piscina* was under way, and the pond, as such was lost. Attempts at drainage of the area were

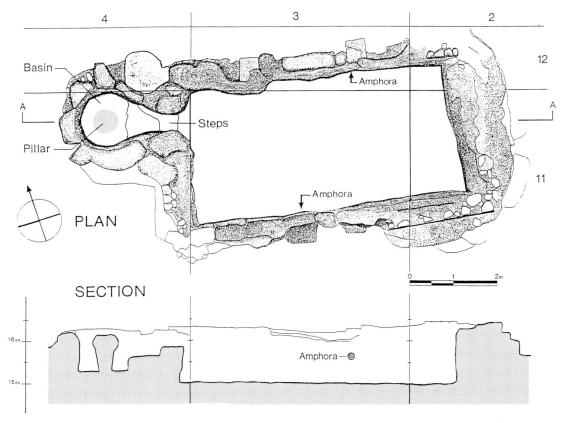

Basin

A ———

Pillar

PLAN

SECTION

4   3   2

12

Amphora

Steps

Amphora

11

A

0   1   2m

16.00

15.00

Amphora —

The *Piscina*

110-111 (above) Piscina *and basin, plan and section, showing pillar and steps of basin, and* amphorae *in the walls of the* piscina. (below) *Body and toe of* amphora *protruding from exterior of wall. Such* amphorae, *with the necks chopped off, were embedded in the walls and used by the fish as places of refuge from light and heat. They provide firm evidence that fish (or eels) inhabited the pool.*

112-114 (above) *Inscription of Sabina. Found in fill near the pool, and therefore out of its original context, the inscription commemorates the great benefactress of the sanctuary in the first century* BC *(see also ill. 94). (right) View from the south. The pool is oddly shaped with the north (far) wall parallel to the stylobate of the Rectangular Hall (beyond), but the south (near) wall not. Thus, the pool is only approximately rectangular. (below) View from the southwest. The lead-lined cutting in the top of the pillar shows that a statuette had stood here and that the pillar's function was ornamental.*

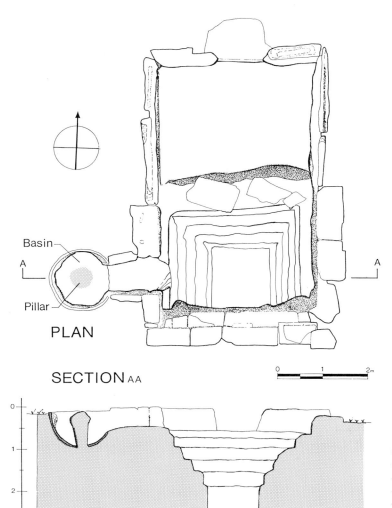

Basin

A ⌐   ⌐ A

Pillar

PLAN

SECTION AA

0   1   2m

115 Sanctuary of Hera, ritual complex, plan and section. This counterpart to the piscina *in the sanctuary at Santa Venera may be seen within the city walls not a stone's throw from the northeast corner of the Temple of Hera II.*

successful to the point that during the second and third centuries AD the earth around the shell of the structure was reworked, and possibly even ploughed. In reworked soil here was found an inscribed marble plaque long lost from its original context hailing Sabina, the great benefactress of the sanctuary in the first century BC. The area was then abandoned until in medieval times (the thirteenth century) a cistern and a kiln testify to activity close by the site of the long forgotten *piscina*.

The connection between the *piscina* and the Hall has already been noted; equally importantly, a complex, similar to the Santa Venera *piscina* may be found, excavated but unpublished, in the sanctuary of Hera within the city walls. About 20 metres from the northeast corner of the Temple of Hera II there appears a parallel feature combining rectangular pools and steps, basin and pillar. Though in this complex the pillar did not obviously carry a statuette (and more erotic uses have been suggested), nor is it necessarily a *piscina* (i.e. no *amphorae* have been found in the walls), it is evident that the Santa Venera *piscina* is closely linked to the principal sanctuary of the ancient city.

The functions of the *piscina* in its heyday were doubtless complex. On a mundane level, it functioned, like its counterparts in Roman gardens, as an aesthetic amenity. The steps leading into the basin imply the presence of humans, and while the fanciful might think of ritual bathing, this seems improbable; the steps perhaps simply facilitated maintenance. In Syria, Atargatis was worshipped as a fish, and in the sanctuary on Samothrace, the fish Pompilos (who showed people the way) was sacred. Closer to home, the Fountain of Arethusa at Syracuse, we are told, nourished the sacred eel: may the *piscina* at Santa Venera have harboured such sacred creatures?

The Divinity

A fragmentary inscription found in earlier excavations had inspired the theory that the sanctuary might have been dedicated to Bona Dea. This is the inscription which speaks of Sabina, the wife of Flaccus, taking care of the reconstruction of the shrine of the goddess (*Deae*), and providing stucco decoration, seats and floors, from her own pocket (*sua pequnia* (see ill. 94)). The broken state of the stone initially allowed the restoration of *Bonae* before *Deae*, and indeed epigraphically such a restoration is possible. New evidence from the Michigan-Perugia excavations, however, renders this appealing restoration, and the hypotheses that would follow, unacceptable.

In the summer of 1983, investigations in the Rectangular Hall produced an inscribed marble base for a statuette; this base was used as a building

116 Inscribed marble base for a statuette with dedication to Venus, third century BC, found in the sanctuary at Santa Venera in 1983. Most of the name of the donor is lost, but there is no doubting the divinity (VENEREI) for whom the gift was intended.

Marble Venus Statuettes

*117-120 (left) half-draped Venus, first century BC.
This statuette is a variant of a famous Hellenistic
type, the Venus Anadyomene (= Venus Rising from
the Sea; which she evidently is not). More accurately
the type might be known as Venus Arranging Her
Hair! (below) Half-draped Venus, first century BC. A
variant of the Leaning Aphrodite type which first
appeared in terracotta in the fourth century BC, this
figure incorporates quotations from another type (the
Venus Marina with which she shares the prominent
triangle of drapery over the knee). Slim proportions
point to the first century BC. (opposite) Draped
Venus with figure on the right shoulder, first century
BC. The largest of the statuettes that have survived
from the sanctuary is a variant of the Aphrodite
Tiepolo type; she leans saucily on a cylindrical pillar,
a small figure perched on her shoulder: was it Eros
or Pothos (= Desire)? Draped Venus, rear view
showing legs (body broken off and lost) of small
figure on the shoulder, details of drapery, right arm
akimbo and left with elbow locked.*

block in the uppermost course of rubble masonry between the two eastern-most niches of Room B. Though broken, the inscription records a dedication to Venus [... *f.Cn. Venerei* (line 1) ... *onavit* (line 2)], and testifies to worship of the goddess. The kind of dative used in the inscription, *Venerei* (the more orthodox is *Veneri*) is early, as is the lettering of the writing, so that the dedication is likely to have taken place shortly after the foundation of the colony in the early third century BC. The letter *f.* is the abbreviation for *filius* (= son), and the donor's father's name is abbreviated to *Cn.* (= Cnaius), with the actual donor's name lost at the beginning of the line. What is interesting here is the arrangement of the formula, the placement of the father's name after the *f.* where we should have expected it the other way

121 Marble statuette of draped Venus, first century BC. Prominent sideways posture, sharp contraposto stance yielding horizontal axis through hips tilting one way and that through the shoulders the other, fingers of hand spread out on the hip with index finger pointing are all stylistic traits and conventions which are at home in the Hellenistic world. Another variant of the Aphrodite Tiepolo type, elongated proportions and simplified drapery point to first century production.

round, i.e. *Cn.f.* There is no parallel to this order of words in the whole of Latin epigraphy: it seems that we have found a dedication made under the influence of some other language than Latin, recorded in Latin conventions newly (and not wholly) learnt. It is worth remembering that the old inhabitants of Poseidonia, Greeks and Lucanians, continued to live in the city, and that Etruscans too may have been co-opted into the colony.

More epigraphic evidence attesting the presence of Venus emerged in 1984: a dozen or so joining sherds of a large Roman redware vessel datable to the first century AD, perhaps a suspension or garden pot, were inscribed with fascinating information. They tell us of the existence of a certain Valerius, a centurion of Venus, *centurio Veneris*, and of slaves of Venus, and we may logically infer that Valerius and the slaves were active in the sanctuary. A parallel *centuria Veneria*, a century of slaves of Venus (more likely in fact about sixty or seventy), is attested, as luck would have it, at nearby Herculaneum, and has been connected with the cult of Venus of Eryx. Thus, it was Venus who was worshipped in this sanctuary in the Roman period, and the Bona Dea theory must be abandoned.

The authority of Venus in this part of Paestum is confirmed by a series of marble statuettes, one at least found by Sestieri in his excavations, and others recovered prior to the construction of the extension to the Cirio Factory in 1957. These statuettes are, alas, headless, but present a formidable gallery of evidence. There is one adaptation of the half-draped Venus Anadyomene type (perhaps found by Sestieri who speaks of a 'torsetto femminile con himation che copriva la sola parte inferiore del corpo' – a headless female statuette with a *himation* (garment) which covered only the lower part of the body'), and examples of two other half-draped Venus types (one a variant of the Leaning Aphrodite type, the other an example of the Aphrodite of Miletus type). There are two draped Venus types (variants of the Aphrodite Tiepolo type) of which one had a small figure of Pothos (= Desire) or Eros on her shoulder. There is one Artemis (or armed Venus?), and one other female, a mortal since she wears a ring on her finger, who may have been a priestess. Among male representations, there is a seated Hermes (who functioned also as a fountain head), a bearded herm, and figure of a youth, perhaps a personification of the Season of Spring. All these figures belong to the first century BC or AD, and all are at home in a sanctuary of Venus. Several of the figures came from a collapsed 'fontana', to judge from notes kindly supplied by the Soprintendenza, located where the Cirio's extension now stands; such a structure would have accounted for the seated Hermes, and for representations of Venus, whether interpreted actually as Venus types or seen by the visitors as Nymphs. Distinctions between Venus types and Nymph types are a constant source of headaches to commentators: it seems the two were more or less interchangeable.

So Venus was the deity honoured here from the third century BC onwards. We are left with the question of her predecessor from the first days of the sanctuary on. The shape of the *oikos* (a circle in a square) finds only a single precise parallel in the whole of Greek architecture, the so-called Heroon at Olympia. The Olympia building is identified as a heroon on the basis of Hellenistic inscriptions, but what of the fifth century BC? In describing the area at Olympia, Pausanias speaks of two places of cult, one for the *Despoinai* (Damia and Auxesia, the west Greek variants of Demeter and Persephone), the other for Aphrodite, the Horai and the Nymphs; may we suggest that in the fifth century the building at Olympia was dedicated to Aphrodite? And that its counterpart at Poseidonia, its major architectural parallel, served the same mistress? Even more compelling is the evidence of the terracotta figurines. Numerous figurines of the Archaic period retrieved from the site at Santa Venera represent female divinities; exceptional among these are no less than twenty-one representations of a nude female deity who can only be Aphrodite. This number is almost double the number of examples of the type found elsewhere in the whole of Poseidonia, and tells us that the sanctuary at Santa Venera was the principal centre for the worship of Aphrodite in the whole city. So it was Aphrodite who was worshipped here from the very beginning; and it is worth recalling that Aphrodite, as the wife of Zeus, was worshipped at Troizen, and that it is exiles originally from Troizen who founded Poseidonia. This Aphrodite Hera or Aphrodite Nymphaia, as she was known, may then have travelled with the settlers who moved from Troizen to Sybaris, and thence, exiled again, to Poseidonia in the very earliest days of the city's life.

122 Terracotta figurine of Aphrodite (nude), sixth century BC. Over twenty of these nude figurines have been found at Santa Venera; 80 per cent more than the number found elsewhere in the whole of Poseidonia, they suggest that this was the city's major sanctuary of Aphrodite.

CHAPTER NINE

DECLINE, DISAPPEARANCE AND DISCOVERY

Late Antiquity

Evidence for Paestum in late Roman and medieval times is regrettably patchy: a somewhat reckless excavation policy, which focused naturally enough on the Greek city, did not in the accustomed methods of the time pay much attention to the late classical remains. So the archaeological report is summary; and there is little written evidence prior to the papal records. Reorganization and reconstruction took place on the south side of the Forum, as we have seen, in the second or third centuries AD, with the building of the *macellum* (the market), and the so-called *curia* (senate house). At the same time, a large bath building was also restored and in the sanctuary of Santa Venera too there was activity in these centuries. But Paestum was entering on a period of steady decline.

The town had long since lost its position of mercantile importance, when the construction of the via Popilia cut her off from the main artery of north-south landborne trade, and when Puteoli became the new focus for maritime entrepreneurs. Strabo remarks in the first century that the sanding up of streams that gave outlet to the sea to the Capodifiume/Salso had already created swamps and that the area was unhealthy. By the first century, then, municipal government was experiencing difficulty keeping open the passages for the springwater to the sea; the unpredictability of these springs, the character of the water and the creeks they formed can only have been a nightmare for local engineers. Many Roman public servants were adept and conscientious when it came to maintaining and controlling water supplies – Frontinus, *curator aquarum* at Rome in the time of the emperor Trajan, is a case in point – but at Paestum it all seems to have become too much. By the third century AD, matters were getting out of hand: alluvial and calcic deposits were choking streams; streams were petrifying and causing flooding, marshes and malaria; anchorages were sanding up with inadequate dredging.

People began to emigrate, and the city contracted: by the fourth century some houses were being used as sites for limekilns, and refuse pits were opened even in the Forum itself – social conventions had broken down, and buildings and spaces were used for new purposes. Yet inscriptions of AD 337 and 347 record the continued existence of magistracies (*duoviri*) and tell of meetings in the *curia* where *decuriones* (senators) and other poohbahs were on hand. From the fifth century on, it seems, houses congregated around the highest point in the landscape – the rise on which stood the Temple of Athena, now converted into a Christian church. The temple's orientation was reversed, burials were allowed in what had been the peristyle, and houses huddled around the newly sanctified structure. To the east, and now visible in its restored form immediately adjacent to the Archaeological Museum, rose the church of the *Annunziata*, making liberal use of looted Roman columns and capitals. No precise information allows speculation about the chronological relationship between these two churches; but a cemetery, datable between the fifth and seventh centuries AD, seems to have extended over a large area, to judge from tombs found both in and outside the Temple of Athena and others outside the church of the *Annunziata* beyond the walls of its apse. The size of this cemetery, and the discovery of medieval walls near the Temples of Hera, together with those near the Temple of Athena perhaps speak for a late antique/early medieval settlement of more generous proportions than has hitherto been thought.

Certainly by the time of Pope Gregory the Great (as witnessed by a letter of AD 599) there is a diocese at Paestum, distinct from that of Agropoli, and there is evident concern for the organization of religious life in the district. The discovery of a large cemetery with burials of the sixth and seventh centuries at S. Marco points to the existence of active communities along this coast at this time. Papal records declare the presence of a bishop of Paestum at a church council in AD 652, but thereafter silence descends. The second half of the seventh century is pretty much of a blank; but that the eyes of Paestans, surviving the insalubrious swamps and vegetation of the plain, were turning eagerly towards the hills behind the city, may be shown by the construction of a church – unless this is the work of a monastic order – on a high outcrop of the mountain some 3 miles (5 km) from the city. This church, directly overlooking the springs of water, the Capodifiume, was built in the eighth century. It was embellished with three apses, two aisles and a nave, and in the course of its life underwent several structural alterations: it doubtless served as the cathedral when the bishopric was transferred towards the end of the ninth century from Paestum to a new town in the hills (Capaccio). Ecclesiastical dependencies – perhaps a bishop's residence – were built nearby, and the area behind the church was used as a cemetery.

The Middle Ages

Capaccio (= *Caput Aquae* = Water Source) is situated on the flanks of the mountain overlooking the plain, and, as its name implies, the Capodifiume. The remains are impressive: several stretches of fortification walls including towers, traces of a baronial residence, and outside the fortified town the cathedral of *Santa Maria del Granato* (Saint Mary of the Pomegranate) built near the eighth-century church. This whole area has been the subject of recent archaeological exploration by teams from the University of Salerno and from the Polish Academy of Sciences. It seems that the earliest medieval dwellings built at the end of the ninth century were of wood, and that a second phase boasted a defensive perimeter around buildings still wood-built; in the final phase rubble masonry was used for houses protected by a fortification wall. It was marauding Saracens who stimulated the creation of Capaccio. Their appearance in the late ninth century struck terror into the hearts of the Paestans. Vulnerable in their coastal location, already disposed to abandon their malaria-ridden town, they were suddenly afflicted by this *furore africano*, as the Saracen raids were called. Many took to the hills; so did the bishop.

Capaccio grew and flourished. The new cathedral of *Santa Maria del Granato* – the obvious heiress of the cult of Hera, since images of the saint follow the iconography of Hera, holding a child on one side, and a pomegranate in the other hand – was built in the twelfth century, adjacent to the earlier eighth-century church. The bishop's palace was rebuilt and the old church performed a new ecclesiastical (liturgical?) function. Though in the twelfth century the city is described as *oppidum munitissimum* (i.e., highly fortified), it could not withstand the assault of Frederick II in AD 1247. Capaccio had become the centre of a baronial revolt, and paid the penalty. There was a long seige; fire and the sword were the order of the day at the last; and most of the citizens were either killed or dispersed. Only the church of Santa Maria del Granato remained standing, while a handful of citizens eked out a precarious living among the ruins of the town.

While Capaccio prospered, the plain was not altogether deserted. If the tenth century may be seen as a time of regrouping, and consolidation, centred now both administratively and economically on Capaccio, the eleventh may be seen as a period of resumption of activity and tentative expansion in the plain. New plots of land were subject to the plough; archaeological evidence appears again and tells of human activity, not clustered in a few specific locales, but dotted about at various locations. In the twelfth century confidence grew as the population multiplied: evidence for actual inhabitation, albeit widely scattered, has come to light, and commerce as well as agriculture takes a hand. Predominant shapes of locally produced pottery (*amphorae, pithoi*) were for storage and transport of agricultural goods, while the discovery of North African and Byzantine wares is good evidence for the resumption of commerce. At Paestum itself, the area around the Temple of Athena was again a centre of activity and has yielded pottery of the twelfth and thirteenth centuries, and coins of similar date.

Much good evidence has been retrieved at Paestum from the *località* Santa Venera, both from the excavations in the sanctuary immediately south of the city wall, and from those in the necropolis further south. Pottery from the necropolis, found discarded in an earlier well, and sherds of imported green glazed wares found in the sanctuary are firm evidence of occupation of this area in the twelfth and thirteenth centuries, and of commerce.

Telling evidence comes from the upper levels in the area of the *piscina* in the sanctuary (see Chapter 8). After a long period of disuse – perhaps as long as 800 years – and at a time when only the very tops of the walls of the now filled-in *piscina* were visible, people went to work. A U-shaped kiln, of which only a single course of masonry survived, was built atop the east wall of the *piscina*, facing west towards the depressed earth within the erstwhile pond (perhaps for ease of access); a rectangular built flue survived at the north, and both flue and kiln contained a lot of ash and carbonized matter. The soil below the kiln was discoloured as a result of heat above; while the encrustation which had taken place many years previously on the interior of the *piscina* wall, directly below the mouth of the kiln, likewise gave evidence of intense heat: a large piece of it had disappeared, burnt off. Two ceramic coarse ware firing stands, of use in the process of firing pots inverted in a kiln, came to light in the adjacent soil. Close by, to the north, the industrious medieval denizens built a circular cistern which cut through the walls both of the pond and of the adjacent pear-shaped basin (a handy intervention, from the standpoint of recent investigations, for deciphering the construction methods of the *piscina* and its basin); deposits of encrustation on the interior show that the cistern had held water at various moments, and its use in harness with the kiln is hardly disputable. Together they tell of industrial activity here. Two sherds of vitreous glazed pottery of thirteenth-century date appeared among the rubble masonry of the kiln itself, while a broken, but almost entirely mendable, vitreous glazed pitcher also of thirteenth-century date – badly burnt, and therefore probably misfired in the kiln – came to light at the bottom of the cistern; two coins of the second half of the thirteenth century also appeared in fill close by. So the chronology is firm.

Further evidence of medieval activity on this site comes from a huge pit directly in the centre of the entrance into Room C of the Rectangular Hall. This pit which measured almost 2 metres in diameter at the top and went all the way down to and cut into the travertine shelf, gave evidence of two periods of deposit: a lower, containing pottery of the first and second centuries AD, datable thence to the third century, and a higher, containing much medieval pottery, datable to the thirteenth or early fourteenth century. The pit probably represents two failed attempts to dig wells, first Roman and then medieval, the cavities created then used for garbage disposal.

Most striking is the evidence of the coins. The excavations in the sanctuary have produced 70 coins to which may be added a further 34 retrieved earlier by Sestieri and Napoli and their colleagues. Of these 104, eight are medieval and all eight are of the thirteenth century; they are issues of Frederick II, Conrad I, Manfred, and Charles of Anjou, minted between AD 1221 and

1285. They appear to be losses of the third and fourth quarters of the thirteenth century. The official listing of the numismatic collections in the Archaeological Museum at Paestum counts only 11 examples from the whole of the ancient city, of the coinage of which Santa Venera alone has produced 8. The 11 examples in the Museum are part of a collection numbering 2,829 coins (1,200 Greek; 1,548 Roman; a mere 81 medieval and modern, down to the nineteenth century). The ratio of medieval coins to others (8:96) from the Santa Venera sanctuary is much higher than that of parallel pieces to others (11:2,748) from the whole of the rest of Poseidonia/Paestum; the incidence of appearance of thirteenth-century medieval coins is much more common. The coins alone would admit the conjecture that the *località* Santa Venera was a principal, if not *the* principal, hub of human life in the thirteenth-century community. If the evidence of the coins is put next to the evidence of the industrial installation on the site of the fishpond, the pottery deposit from the pit in the Rectangular Hall, and the rich materials from the cemetery to the south, the conclusion is hardly disputable.

Disappearance

For the later fourteenth century, there is as yet little evidence, and the only clear archaeological materials from the fifteenth and sixteenth centuries come from – of all places – the site of the sanctuary of Hera at Foce del Sele: there, traces of a modest but continuing settlement have been found. The bishops of Capaccio no longer resided at Capaccio, but held court at various locations, sometimes at Salerno, or at Novi or at Sala. In the late sixteenth century one episcopal tenant described Capaccio as utterly destroyed with the exception of the church of S. Maria del Granato which still functioned – *pulchra moenibus ... et quotidie una missa celebrata* ('beautiful in its walls ... and a mass is celebrated daily'): he goes on to record that the bishops had not lived there for a long while, but lived in the diocese *ubi sibi placet* ('where they pleased').

The decrepitude of the diocese continued in the next century, and little seemingly was done to prevent the slow erosion of any church presence. Bishop Carafa reported in 1644: *situs ipsius asperrimus, montibus praecelsis, imis vallibus, silvis et nemoribus, fluvis et paludibus impeditus* – ('the area is very rugged, inaccessible by reason of lofty mountains, precipitous valleys, forests and woods, rivers and marshes'). He paints a picture of an inhospitable landscape through which it was difficult for a bishop to make his way; the aptitude for security which prompted the removal of the bishopric from Paestum to Capaccio in the ninth century no longer presented a valid reason for visiting, let alone residing at, Capaccio. Moreover, the locals were hostile: another wrote, in 1682, that *populi istius diocesis indomiti, feroces, ad arma promptissimi* – ('the people of that diocese are out of control, wild, most ready to violence'). If these reports are to be believed, brigandage was rife, with more people living and lurking in the woods than on the land. Small wonder that the authority of the church, or any authority for that matter, was at a low ebb; and small wonder that bishops and their retinues steered clear.

These descriptions of the countryside and its population hardly chime with reports from other sources, most of which admittedly emanate from the next century. It is fair to say, however, that Bouchard, who visited Naples for nine months in 1632, went often to Salerno and was a devoted philhellene, knew nothing of Poseidonia/Paestum (or he would have remarked on it), and that visitors to Naples in the first half of the eighteenth century were interested principally in the baroque architecture of Naples herself, and in the dramatic qualities and natural beauty of the Campi Flegrei. Poseidonia was largely ignored. But it was not the difficulties of the terrain which preserved the site's isolation. The English traveller, Smith, writing in 1733, describes the journey to Paestum as negotiable in eight days and the road as a good one. The crossing of the Sele would have presented a moment of excitement – there was a ferry – but no more so than many other Italian river crossings in the south as in the north; and there was a bridge at Eboli. People's attention was fixed more on Naples and her glories, and in archaeological terms, on the discovery of Herculaneum in 1738 and the opening of the excavations at Pompeii in 1748.

Discovery

The opportunities for architectural vandalism offered by Paestum were, however, grasped by the eminent Neapolitan architect, Ferdinando Sanfelice, who in 1740 proposed to King Charles of Bourbon, who had inherited the Kingdom of the Two Sicilies in 1734, that columns and other architectural members from the ruins at Paestum should be used to decorate the new structures at Capodimonte; happily, this proposal came to nothing. But serious attention – if for lamentable purposes – had been drawn to the town. Another with an interest in antiquity who saw Paestum with rather different eyes was Count Felice Gazzola. A brilliant courtier and military man, Gazzola was also a devotee of the arts, and Paestum's rediscovery – if it may justly be so called – in the eighteenth century owes much to his efforts. Acquainted with the site through his participation in hunting parties orchestrated by the king in the forests of Persano close to Paestum, Gazzola was so taken by the ruins that in the period between 1745 and 1750 he planned a project which would make drawings not only of the temples but of all other visible monuments. This was to be part of a grandiose scheme which would document all the sites of Magna Graecia, and some of the best minds and hands of Naples of the day were employed in it, notably Gian Battista Natali and Antonio Magri. Gazzola was well-known and liked in Naples, and he was a generous man. News of the project and of Paestum's untapped riches spread. Gazzola's diplomatic and courtly career then took him to Madrid and he was unable to see to the publication of the drawings he had commissioned; they did not in fact appear until they were published by Paoli in 1784.

James Bruce, the discoverer of the Nile, was in Italy in 1762 and 1763, and he too evinced an interest in Paestum after meeting Gazzola and purchasing drawings of the temples from him. He hired Magri in Naples to go with him to Paestum and execute drawings; a copy of these was sold by Magri to a certain John Horne-Tooke in 1765. Other draughtsmen and architects were making their way to Paestum at midcentury, the most famous and influential of whom was J. G. Soufflot, the greatest French architect of the century, who made drawings of the buildings on his visit in 1750 and could not help but express surprise at how little attention was paid in Naples to Paestum. Soufflot's drawings were first published in Paris by G. F. M. Dumont in 1764. In 1768 there appeared in London Thomas Major's *Ruins of Paestum*, dedicated to John Brudenell Montagu, who had himself been fascinated by Paestum on his visit in 1756. Whose drawings did Major use?

John Horne-Tooke – plain John Horne until he underwent hyphenation in 1782 – was an Englishman living in Naples in 1765 and tutoring the son of a certain Mr Taylor. A fellow of discernment, there is every likelihood that he made his drawings available to Major, and one plate of Major's book has the name of Magri on it. Soufflot's drawings were already published in 1764, and were perhaps known to Major even prior to their publication. Recent scholarship has examined the original drawings for Thomas Major's engravings now housed in London at the Sir John Soane Museum, and draws attention to the list of drawings at the beginning of the book: this is handwritten, and with reference to the plans of the temples, declares, 'From a drawing of Capt. S. Rious by Mons. J. G. Soufflot'. Evidently Rious got the drawing from Soufflot, or copied one of Soufflot's drawings; transmission to Major was the next step.

That Major drew on Soufflot is shown by a comparison of the plates in his volume (1768) with those of Soufflot (1764). But this was not copying; alterations and refinements were introduced especially with reference to drawings of elevations. Major's handwritten list of the drawings identifies the draughtsman who made some of these corrections – Mr Robt. Mylne; indeed the initials RM are to be found at the lower left of one of the restored elevations. Mylne was another of those intellectual and aesthetic explorers who made the pilgrimage to Paestum in midcentury (1756). Some of the variations from Soufflot's drawings introduced by Mylne are considerable and he was apparently pulling together Soufflot's work (from Riou) and Magri's work (from Horne) with his own. Major had the work of all three – Soufflot, Magri and Mylne – before him when he produced his masterful amalgamation: he engraved the drawings, he wrote an explanatory text including historical and numismatic comments, he paid his respects, in the

123 Temple of Hera II, engraving by Thomas Major, 1768. Note the combination of romantic (clouds, trees, foliage) and scientific (architect and draughtsman at work) elements, characteristic of the mid-eighteenth century.

124 Temple of Athena, engraving by Thomas Major, 1768. Note the projecting blocks of the horizontal cornice, for which there is no archaeological evidence. Did Major or Major's source confuse their drawings?

preface, to Soufflot; and the volume was presented to an admiring public – and a distinguished list of subscribers – long before the purported competition (Gazzola and company) got their act together.

The new interest in the temples at Paestum provoked, in the best tradition of the Enlightenment, a re-examination of the field of ancient architecture. Heretofore, the tumbled columns of Doric temples, whether seen in Sicily or Greece, were viewed in a spirit of romantic and distant antiquarianism with little to suggest the need for comparison with the ideal of Roman architecture. It was the good fortune of the Paestum temples that they were brought into intellectual focus at the same time as other developments tending to a reassessment of ancient architecture: for example, the publication of Wood's *Ruins of Baalbek* (1757), and Stuart and Revett's *Antiquities* (1762). In a very real sense Paestum was the catalyst for the great debate which then began. Were Greek temples of the Doric Order, with their lack of or understated ornamentation, to be seen as primitive architecture, crude if powerful, without connection to the Roman ideal, embodied in the editions of Vitruvius?

The extent to which Vitruvius' *dicta* controlled early eighteenth-century architectural thought may be seen in the wholly inaccurate elevations of the Parthenon in Athens published at this time. Distortion in the interest of conformity with the principles of Vitruvius was wholeheartedly endorsed; the Parthenon was shown with precipitous pediment, metopes at corners of the frieze, and columns standing on bases. Now, with Paestum within striking distance of Naples, there was a chance to compare the prescriptions of Vitruvius with Greek buildings actually on the Italian mainland. At once Vitruvius was shown to be inaccurate; and the discussion turned to the merits of structure and ornament, to the clarity and propriety of Greek Doric and the decorative insistence of the Roman Late Baroque tradition. Roman architecture was considered autonomous, bolstered by Vitruvius himself, and its superiority indisputable: if precursors were to be sought, they were Etruscan. But new commentators began to stress the simplicity and nobility of the Greek ideal, and to challenge Vitruvian dogma.

This intellectual hubbub was only quieted down by the work of the great German theorist Winckelmann. He visited Paestum in 1760, and like Soufflot a decade earlier was astonished at the lack of interest aroused by the temples; or rather by the contrast between the previous total ignorance of the site and the burgeoning interest – historical, architectural, aesthetic, numismatic. He took the Paestum temples as the starting point for his *Anmerkungen zur Baukunst der Alten* – 'Remarks on the Architecture of the Ancients', rejected Vitruvius' theories and took the buildings themselves as the fundamental evidence. He analyzed and classified; he proposed a new theory of the history of architecture, namely that Greek architectural form was the origin of all later architectural form, and consequently that Roman sprang, grew and developed from Greek. At the same time he underscored the originality of some aspects of Roman architecture and attempted to reconcile the two. Winckelmann's was a work of genius; its publication marked a watershed, and has influenced all subsequent thinking.

Strong support for Winckelmann's new thinking about Doric architecture came eventually from an unlikely source, and was the stronger for it. G. B. Piranesi at first resisted the new view, adhering to the old notions of Roman primacy, the inviolability of Vitruvius' thought about evolution, and the centrality of Etruscan architectural form in the development of Roman. But it was his glorious set of views of the Paestum temples, made towards the end of his life and completed by his son, which put the stamp of approval on the new ideas, and which guaranteed widespread knowledge of the buildings and their importance. The hidden truth, though rendered by Soufflot and intellectually disentangled by Winckelmann, was at last out in the open, brought to life by Piranesi's engravings.

The original builders of the Greek temples at Poseidonia can hardly have imagined the furor that their buildings would create 2,000 and more years later, or that they would have continued into the late twentieth century as abiding documents of early Greek energy and commitment. That they did spark one of the major architectural controversies of the eighteenth century, and that they continue to this day to excite the admiration of tourist and student alike, is testament enough to the creative and imaginative powers of Greek thinkers and builders in Poseidonia more than twenty-four centuries ago.

Visiting Paestum

Paestum is often busy with clamouring tourists or groups of schoolchildren enjoying day excursions, especially in the summer months, but the site is open from dawn to dusk, and it is best if possible to plan to stay overnight and enjoy the monuments both in the early morning and late evening.

The Site

Paestum (*see ill. 3*) is accessible from the road which bisects the ancient city at two points: opposite the Temple of Hera II, giving a full-frontal view of the building at the far side of a carefully tended rose garden, and close to the east end of the Temple of Athena. Sometimes entrance is also possible from the south directly onto the *cardo maximus* immediately north of Nettuno's restaurant.

A circular tour is recommended, beginning from the Temple of Hera II, moving from the southern sanctuary by way of the Forum and its adjacent buildings, the Amphitheatre and the so-called Gymnasium, to the zone of the Greek Agora with the Bouleuterion and the Underground Shrine, and concluding at the Temple of Athena. You may wander some way among the Roman houses to the west, but guards will be aroused if you climb on walls; look out too for snakes, mostly harmless, in the less frequently visited parts. A visit may take between one and three hours depending on enthusiasm and the heat. Add another hour if you choose to walk briskly round the city walls. July and August are hot; spring (April and May) and autumn (October and November) are most promising.

After the visit to the site, the Bar Museo, with every kind of refreshment and genial company, should not be missed; the ice cream, even by Italian standards, is exceptional, and the coffee does more than restore the tissues. Refreshed you may now visit the museum next door (open from 9 AM to 1 PM; closed Mondays and Holidays); the metopes from Foce del Sele are alone worth the visit, but don't miss the painted panels from the Tomb of the Diver and the Lucanian tomb paintings. There is a small charge for admission to the site which also covers entrance to the museum. Lunch at Nettuno's close to the Porta Giustizia, will be a treat to remember. Or, the Ristorante Museo (like the Bar Museo, next door to the museum) offers meals less punishing to the wallet, while the small general store next door will provide sandwiches and soft drinks. Books, guides, newspapers, cards and souvenirs are available in the string of shops which face the site.

How to Get There and Where to Stay

Visits from Naples, the Amalfi coast, and Ravello may easily be made by car within a couple of hours' journey. From Naples the excellent Italian train service takes you right to Paestum – a change of trains at Salerno may be necessary. Once off the train at Paestum, you are within a stone's throw of the fortification walls and the East Gate (Porta Sirena) of the city. From Rome, take a *rapido* (a fast train; the most convenient is called the Peloritano) to Salerno, and you can be in Paestum within four hours; if a local train is not due for the run from Salerno to Paestum, there are numerous buses all day (called Pullmans). By car from Rome airport, take the ring road to the turn-off for the southbound autostrada (A2); from the A2 take the A30 at Caserta which will bypass Naples to the east of Vesuvius, and Salerno. Take the Pontecagnano exit for Paestum; the journey takes about four hours. The Sea Garden Hotel with parking facilities, close to the south wall of the city is convenient and comfortable. Another good and convenient hotel is the nearby Villa Rita, though this is not always open.

Nearby Sites

There is almost nothing to be seen at the Heraion at Foce del Sele today, though the secondary road from Paestum to Salerno along the coast, goes very close to the site. A visit to the Church of the Madonna of the Pomegranate and to Capaccio Vecchio on the slope of the hills behind Paestum yields splendid views over the plain, and is worth a rapid visit. Agropoli is a bustling market town, crowded in summer, as are the countless camping sites at or close to the seashore at Paestum itself; it may be best to avoid July and August if at all possible. Eminently worth a visit is the site of Velia, about an hour to the south, with its Greek acropolis (temple foundations, walls of polygonal masonry elsewhere, modern Museum) well-preserved ancient roadways, and public buildings of both Greek and Roman date. These excursions require the use of a car.

Bibliography

A general bibliography on Poseidonia-Paestum compiled by P. Zancani-Montuoro may be found in *Enciclopedia dell'Arte Antica*, 1963.

Books

ARDOVINO, A.M., *I culti di Paestum antica e del suo territorio*, Naples 1986

BÉRARD, J., *La Colonisation grecque de l'Italie méridionale et de la Sicile dans l'antiquité, l'histoire, et la légende*, Paris 1957

CIPRIANI, M., *San Nicola di Albanella. Scavo di un santuario campestre nel territorio di Poseidonia-Paestum*, in press

CORDANO, F., *Antiche Fondazioni Greche. Sicilia e Italia Meridionale*, 1986

DUNBABIN, T.J., *The Western Greeks*, Oxford 1948

EDLUND, I., *The Gods and the Place*, Stockholm 1987

GRECO, E. and D. THEODORESCU, *Poseidonia-Paestum* I, Rome 1980

GRECO, E. and D. THEODORESCU, *Poseidonia-Paestum* II, Rome 1983

GRECO, E. and D. THEODORESCU, *Poseidonia-Paestum* III, Rome 1985

GRECO, E. and M. TORELLI, *Storia dell'urbanistica. Il mondo greco*, Bari 1983

GRECO, E., A STAZIO and G. VALLET, eds., *Paestum*, Taranto 1987

HACKENS, T., N.D. HOLLOWAY and R.R. HOLLOWAY, eds., *Crossroads of the Mediterranean*, Louvain & Providence 1983

JOHANNOWSKY, W., *Paestum*, Novara 1980

KRAUSS, F. and R. HERBIG, *Der korintisch-dorische Tempel am Forum von Paestum*, Berlin 1939

KRAUSS, F., *Die griechischen Tempel*, Berlin 1941

KRAUSS, F., *Paestum. Die griechischen Tempel. Dritte, erweiterte Auflage*, Berlin 1976

MELLO, M. and G. VOZA, *Le iscrizioni latine di Paestum*, Naples 1968

MERTENS, D., *Der Tempel von Segesta und die dorische Tempelbaukunst des griechischen Westens in Klassicher Zeit*, Mainz 1984

MONTUORO, P, ZANCANI and U. ZANOTTI BIANCO, *Heraion alla foce del Sele*, I-II, Rome 1951–1954

NAPOLI, M., *La Tomba del Tuffatore. La scoperta della grande pittura greca*, Bari 1970

NAPOLI, M., *Paestum*, Novara 1970

PEDLEY, J.G., M. TORELLI and others, *The Extramural Sanctuary in the località Santa Venera at Paestum*, I, in press

RIDGWAY, D., *L'Alba della Magna Grecia*, Milan 1984

SERRA, J. RASPI, ed., *Paestum and the Doric Revival 1750–1830*, Florence 1986

SESTIERI, P.C., *Paestum*, Rome 1968

TRENDALL, A.D., *The Red-figured Vases of Paestum*, Oxford 1987

TRENDALL, A.D., *Red Figure Vases of South Italy and Sicily*, London and New York 1989

VAN KEUREN, F., *The Hera I Temple at Foce del Sele: Reinterpretations of the Metopes and a New Reconstruction of the Frieze*, in press

Various authors, *Il Museo di Paestum. Appunti per una lettura critica del percorso espositivo*, Agropoli 1986

WOODHEAD, A.G. *The Greeks in the West*, London 1962

Articles and Chapters

ARDOVINO, A.M. 'Nuovi oggetti sacri con iscrizioni in alfabeto acheo', *Archeologia Classica* 32 (1980–1983) 65–7

AVAGLIANO, G., 'Paestum, Necropoli di Ponte di Ferro', *Rassegna Storica Salernitana* 2:1 (1985) 261–8

BANDINELLI, R. BIANCHI, rev. M. NAPOLI. *La Tomba del Tuffatore. La scoperta della grande pittura greca* (Bari 1970) in *Dialoghi di Archeologia* 4–5 (1970–1971) 135–42

CRAWFORD, M., 'Paestum and Rome: The Form and Function of a Subsidiary Coinage', in *La Monetazione di Bronzo di Poseidonia-Paestum* (Rome 1973) 47–109

d'AGOSTINO, B., 'Le sirene, il tuffatore e le porte dell'Ade', *Annali del Seminario di studi del mondo classico. Sezione di archeologia e storia antica* 4 (1982) 43–50

FIAMMENGHI, C.A., 'La necropoli romana di S. Marco di Castellabate', *Rassegna Storica Salernitana* 2:1 (1985) 269–77

FRASCHETTI, A., 'Aristosseno, i Romani e la barbarizzazione di Poseidonia' *Aion* III (1981) 97ff.

GRAHAM, A.J., 'The Western Greeks', *Cambridge Ancient History*² III, 163–95

GRECO, E., 'Il TEIXOS dei Sibariti e le origini di Poseidonia', *Dialoghi di Archeologia* 8:1 (1974–1975) 104–15

GRECO, E., 'La ceramica arcaica di Poseidonia', in *Il commercio greco nel Tirreno in eta arcaica* (Salerno 1981) 57–66

GRECO, E., 'Non morire in citta: annotazioni sulla necropoli del "Tuffatore" di Poseidonia', *Annali del Seminario di studi del mondo classico. Sezione di archeologia e storia antica* 4 (1982) 51–6

GRECO, E., 'Poseidonia entre le VIe et le IIe siècle avant J-C: quelques problèmes de topographie historique,' *Revue Archéologique* (1979:2) 219–34

GRECO, E., 'Qualche riflessione ancora sulle origini di Poseidonia', *Dialoghi di Archeologia* 1:2 (1979) 51–6

GRECO, E., 'Richerche sulla *chora* poseidoniate: il "paesaggio agrario" dalla fondazione della citta alla fine del sec. IV a.C.', *Dialoghi di Archeologia* 1:2 (1979) 7–26

GUARDUCCI, M., 'Dedica arcaica all Hera di Poseidonia', *Archeologia Classica* 4 (1952) 150–2

GULLINI, G., 'Urbanistica e Architettura', in *Megale Hellas* (Milan 1983) 226–37, 270–6, 304–10

HOERSCHELMANN, S. GRUNAUER VON, 'Die Bronzeprägung von Poseidonia', in *La Monetazione di Bronzo di Poseidonia-Paestum* (Rome 1973) 25–45

JOHANNOWSKY, W., J.G. PEDLEY and M. TORELLI, 'Excavations at Paestum 1982', *American Journal of Archaeology* 87 (1983) 293–303

MELLO, M., 'Strabo V 4.13 e le origini di Poseidonia', *La Parola del Passato* 22 (1967) 402ff.

MONTUORO, P. ZANCANI, 'Hera Hippia', *Archeologia Classica* 13 (1961) 31–9

PEDLEY, J.G. and M. TORELLI, 'Excavations at Paestum 1983', *American Journal of Archaeology* 88 (1984) 367–76

PEDLEY, J.G., 'Excavations at Paestum 1984' *American Journal of Archaeology* 89 (1985) 53–60

PONTRANDOLFO, A. GRECO and A. ROUVERET, 'Ideologia funeraria e societa a Poseidonia nel IV secolo a.C.', in *La Mort, les morts dans les sociétés anciennes* (Cambridge 1982) 299–317

PONTRANDOLFO, A. GRECO, 'Segni di trasformazioni sociali a Poseidonia tra la fine del V e gli inizi del III sec. a.C.', *Dialoghi di Archeologia* 1:2 (1979) 27–50

PRISCO, G., 'Tra economia e societa: la moneta e la tomba a Poseidonia', *Annali dell'Istituto Italiano di Numismatico* (1985) 23–56

SESTIERI, P.C., 'Iconographie et culte d'Héra à Paestum', *Revue des Arts* (1955) 152–7

SESTIERI, P.C., 'Le origini di Poseidonia alla luce delle recenti scoperte di Palinuro', *Archeologia Classica* 2 (1950) 183–4

SESTIERI, P.C., 'Ricerche poseidoniati', *Mélanges de l'école Française de Rome* 67 (1955) 37–48

TORELLI, M., 'C. Cocceius Flaccus, senatore di Paestum, Mineia M.F. e Bona Mens', *Annali della Facolta di Lettere e Filosofia*, Universita degli Studi di Perugia 18:1 (1980–1981) 103–16

List of Illustrations

All colour plates are by Aaron Levin who was also responsible for most of the black-and-white photographs (Levin photographs copyright 1990 Aaron M. Levin).

Illustrations 84, 89, 90, 94–98, 108 are by Sue Webb; 45 is by Rebecca Miller Ammerman; 44 (also the *frontispiece*) and 74 are by Roger J.A. Wilson; 2, 4 and 71 are from the sources cited. All objects photographed are in the Paestum Museum and appear by generous courtesy of the Museum and the Soprintendenza.

Drawings 1, 3, 6, 7, 8, 18, 19, 27, 34, 49, 60, 76 are by David Bosse and Mary Pedley, from the sources cited; 9, 85, 87, 93, 101, 104, 105, 106, 110, and 115 are by David Myers. Other drawings are from the sources cited, the use of which is gratefully acknowledged.

Colour plates

AFTER PAGE 44

I Via Sacra, from the south.
II Temple of Hera I, from the east.
III Temple of Hera II, from the west.
IV Temple of Hera II, interior.
V Temple of Athena, from the northwest.
VI Temple of Athena, interior, from the east.

AFTER PAGE 84

VII Tomb of the Diver, underside of coffin lid.
VIII Tomb of the Diver, figures at the banquet.
IX Sixth-century BC terracotta figurine of Hera Hippia.

AFTER PAGE 102

X Lucanian tomb painting: return of the warrior.
XI Lucanian tomb painting: Charon ferrying passenger over the Styx.

Monochrome illustrations

Frontispiece: Surviving metope from Temple in sanctuary at Foce del Sele.
1 Map of southern Italy and Sicily in Greek period. (adapted from J. Boardman, *The Greeks Overseas*, 1980; p. 160).

2 Aerial view of Paestum, from north. (from G. Gullini, *Megale Hellas*, Milan, 1986; fig. 228).
3 Plan of excavations within city walls. (adapted from W. Johannowsky, *Paestum*, 1980; p. 18).
4 Aerial view of Paestum. (from J. Bradford, *Ancient Landscapes; studies in field archaeology*, London, 1957; pl. 52).
5 Eighteenth-century engraving of city from east gate. (from T. Major, *The Ruins of Paestum*, 1768; pl. 3).
6 Map showing Paestum and surrounding territory. (adapted from E. Greco, 'Poseidonia entre le VIe et le IVe siècle avant J.-C.' *Revue Archéologique*, 1979:2; p. 229).
7 Map of Greece and Aegean coasts. (adapted from J. Boardman, *The Greeks Overseas*, 1980; p. 22).
8 Plan of Paestum and immediate environs. (adapted from A.D. Trendall, *The Red–figured Vases of Paestum*, 1987, and E. Greco, A. Stazio, G. Vallet (eds.), *Paestum*, 1987; pl. 13).
9 Diagrams of strata of sanctuary in the *località* Santa Venera.
10 Channel cut outside sanctuary wall, exposing strata.
11 Sixty-century BC Underground Shrine, from southwest.
12 Sixth-century BC bronze hydria from Shrine.
13 Sixth-century BC Attic black-figure amphora from Shrine.
14 Sixth-century BC silver coin of Poseidonia.
15 Sixth-century BC terracotta figurine of Hera Kourotrophos.
16 Sixth-century BC terracotta figurine of Hera Hoplosmia.
17 View of Temple of Hera I.
18 Plan of Temple of Hera I. (adapted from M. Napoli, *Paestum*, Novara, 1976; p. 5).
19 Drawing of typical Doric temple elevation. (adapted from G. Gullini, *Megale Hellas*, Milan, 1986; pl. 23).
20 Detail of Hera I capital.
21 Detail of Hera I west façade interior.
22 Part of architectural terracotta figure from Temple of Hera I?
23 Interior of Temple of Hera I, from west.
24 Columns between *antae* of Hera I porch.
25 Inscribed silver disk found in Hera I sanctuary.
26 Detail of *anta* capital of Hera I porch.
27 Plan of Temple of Athena. (adapted from G. Gruben *et al*, *Greek Temples, Theaters and Shrines*, New York, 1962; p. 411).

Index

Numbers in *italic* refer to illustration numbers